No Heavy Lifting

No Heavy Lifting

Globetrotting
Adventures
of a Sports
Media Guy

Rob Simpson

Foreword by
John Shannon

Library and Archives Canada
Cataloguing in Publication

Simpson, Rob, 1964–, author
No heavy lifting : globetrotting
adventures of a sports media
guy / Rob Simpson.

Includes bibliographical references.
Issued in print and electronic formats.
ISBN 978-1-77041-434-1 (softcover).
also ISSUED AS: 978-1-77305-204-5 (PDF),
978-1-77305-203-8 (EPUB)

1. Simpson, Rob, 1964– —Anecdotes.
2. Simpson, Rob, 1964– —Travel.
3. Sportscasters—United States—
Anecdotes. 4. Sports—United
States—Anecdotes. I. Title.

GV742.42.S56A3 2018   070.4'49796092
C2017-906599-8   C2017-906600-5

Editor for the press: Michael Holmes
Cover design: David A. Gee
Cover and author photo: © Jen Squires/
www.jensquiresphotographer.com

All photos are from the author's personal
collection.

The publication of *No Heavy Lifting* has been generously supported by the Government
of Canada through the Canada Book Fund. *Ce livre est financé en partie par le
gouvernement du Canada.* We also acknowledge the contribution of the Government
of Ontario through the Ontario Book Publishing Tax Credit and the Ontario Media
Development Corporation.

Ontario
Ontario Media Development
Corporation

Canada

RECYCLED
Paper made from
recycled material
FSC® C103560

PRINTED AND BOUND IN CANADA BY NORECOB   5 4 3 2 1

To Pete Bowers and Ric Blackwell
— broadcasting legends in my world

PREFACE

This is not "I was born a tall white child . . ." I'm not famous, so I do not warrant a memoir. These are individual episodes — the wired, wacky, weird, and wonderful — related to working as a broadcaster around the world.

A couple of notes: for my Yankee friends, it's written with Canadian English; for example, labor and honor read as labour and honour. For my Canuck friends, and some Yanks, there is plenty of behind-the-scenes NHL insight and intrigue going on.

One other thing: kind of weird for a book made of paper, where you can't clip and paste, but I've added a

YouTube link at the bottom of many chapters. Just type the provided title in the YouTube search bar and you'll see a cool short video directly related to the material or a brief video version of the material itself.

I'm putting my thank-yous here. Thank you, John Shannon, for the support over the years, the kind words, and for writing the foreword even though I don't think you've seen the non-hockey chapters. Pete Bowers started me down this road in high school; Ric Blackwell made sure I stayed on it. Thank you to the late Bill Kreifeldt (1941–2016), who gave a trio of teenage reporters their first NBA media credentials. Thank you Ernie Harwell and Bruce Martyn for providing inspiration.

Thank you, Michael Holmes, David Caron, Jack David, editor Laura Pastore, and the entire hard-working posse at ECW. Thank you to dear friend and independent editor Karen Milner.

This isn't about me. It's about the stories. I hope you enjoy it.

— *Simmer*

FOREWORD

BY JOHN SHANNON

I have often been quoted as saying that hockey succeeds in spite of itself. Its greatest attribute isn't the speed or athletic ability required to play the game. Nor is it the sounds of the game or its physical nature. Hockey succeeds because of the people in and around the game and the stories they tell.

This book is a great example of that.

I first heard of Rob Simpson as the play-by-play voice of the Boardwalk Bullies of the East Coast Hockey League (ECHL). They were a short-lived franchise that won the league championship only to disappear almost as quickly as they appeared. The team could only wish to have the same shelf life and passion for hockey as Rob Simpson. You see, Simpson isn't that run-of-the-mill guy who works on the fringes of the game (like the rest of us in the media). He is a passionate survivor. He sees things in the game that many do not. He is able to dissect why people play this great game at any level, from peewee to pro, from Chattanooga to China. He sees and respects the game at any and every level.

Over the last two decades, I have hired Rob for at least three jobs. It was never boring with him around. Make no mistake about it, Rob can be a pain in the ass. He is relentless in his pursuit of what makes hockey so important to so many people. He believes in the game so much that he expects others to believe in and understand it as well. It is a blessing and a curse.

What is endearing about Rob is his ability to find a story in the minutiae of sport or, rather, those people in sport. And as you will read, his love of competition and athletes goes beyond hockey: he has an innate ability to look beyond the competition to find the humorous, the eccentric, even the emotional side to a competitor's story. That's what makes Rob what he is: an excellent storyteller.

With that in mind, sit back, relax, and enjoy the ride. And know that Rob Simpson makes every journey well worth the time.

"Running with the children the other morning
. . . I'll be touched and remember forever."

Steve Montador, a few days after visiting
a school in the Serengeti, June 2007

MONTY

Steve Montador took a lot of punches. He wasn't the most successful hockey fighter, but he was always a willing participant. Willing to stick up for any teammate; willing to drop the mitts at the appropriate time. He would best be considered a middleweight who often fought heavyweight enforcers. He fought stars, shit disturbers, and grinders. According to hockeyfights.com, in his career, "Monty" fought fifty-one different NHLers, nine of them multiple times, and, based on the visual evidence, lost the majority of his fights.

But whether he won or lost at fisticuffs meant little. A hard-working defenceman, he played the game the right way and was cherished by any man wearing the same sweater.

He was also freaking hilarious.

The longest, hardest sustained laughter I have experienced as an adult occurred while listening to Montador tell a story about laser hair removal in a sensitive area of his body and the interactions with the middle-aged woman who was removing it. We were sitting at a remote resort restaurant on the shores of the Indian Ocean, north of Dar es Salaam, Tanzania, eating dinner with Andrew Ference, his former teammate in Calgary and at the time a Boston Bruins defenceman; as well as Mark Brender, then Canadian Deputy Director of the humanitarian sports organization Right To Play; Patrick Gamere, our videographer from New England Sports Network (NESN); and our local cab driver, whom we invited to sit and join us despite the fact he spoke only Swahili.

The cabbie didn't need to speak English to know that Monty's story was outrageously funny. Simply watching Monty's gestures and the rest of us doubled over, the cabbie was laughing, eyes watering, as hard as the rest of us.

It was one of the many times the man had us in stitches during a trip that had its fair share of very serious moments. Like when the machine gun–toting Tanzanian cop decided whether or not he was going to let our van pass through his checkpoint; when we almost stepped on not one but two very deadly eastern green mamba snakes in the Serengeti; when some remote villagers may have taken exception to us not buying any of their handmade goods after welcoming us like kings; and when we regularly realized just how amazing the local children were, despite the fact they were dealing with crushing poverty, AIDS, and abuse.

Monty was there on a mission with Ference to learn first-hand about the work of Right To Play in East Africa and to pass that knowledge and experience along to potential supporters back home. I was helping that effort by producing and hosting an hour-long documentary on their almost week-long adventure for NHL Network TV and also a couple of half-hour versions for NESN.

They were long days full of smiles, enlightenment, and inspiration while playing games with Tanzanian children, followed by deeper reflection on a nightly basis. The reality of the kids' living conditions and lifestyle was humbling and confounding.

Montador had committed to the trip just a week before it began, after another NHL hockey player, Georges Laraque, then of the Penguins, backed out due to a summer training injury. On day two, Andrew described his appreciation of Monty's effort.

"It's pretty cool that a guy can come on a big trip to Africa with six days' notice. There aren't too many guys around who would do that but . . . let alone come with the enthusiasm and understanding about what Right To Play is all about. He really is just opening his arms to what we're seeing here, and the culture here, and what we're all about."

Right To Play uses games and sports in places like sub-Saharan Africa to teach kids life lessons they normally wouldn't be exposed to. Not only do children show up to school in greater numbers during these RTP activity days, so do more teachers. Among other things, the activities teach the kids about avoiding malaria, protecting themselves against HIV, and treating others, especially girls and women in this otherwise very patriarchal landscape, with respect.

Ference and Montador flew overnight from London to Dar es Salaam, met us at the Peacock Hotel City Centre, and within an hour were in a van heading to the first venue, an orphanage, or *dogo dogo* ("little" in Swahili), somewhere in the middle of the city. We had no idea where we were going; we relied on a full-time Tanzanian guide named Leila Sheik, hired by the local Right To Play office, to get us everywhere.

She got us past the cops, made sure our meals and hotel rooms were taken care of, negotiated with villagers, and basically saved our asses whenever we were clueless or potentially in trouble. (I was happy to see Leila pop up on Twitter in June 2015. After our trip in 2007, we thought there was a strong possibility she might get killed. She was a pretty mouthy anti-government activist, who at one point told a hotel manager to go F himself.)

Leila referred to Andrew and Steve, these athlete ambassadors, as *her stars* — "Whatever my stars want, my stars get."

On day one, Leila's stars got a dose of reality. The *dogo dogo* was a part-time school, part-time recreation centre, and full-time housing facility, teeming with abused kids and AIDS orphans. The country has millions of them. Half of the population lives below the poverty line; most adults earn the equivalent of about US$200 a year.

Issac, literally the first kid we met, was wearing a white

t-shirt that had a photograph printed on the front of Steve Yzerman hoisting the Stanley Cup after the Detroit Red Wings won it in 1997. Isaac didn't know Steve Yzerman's name, nor would he know Wayne Gretzky or Gordie Howe. He wouldn't know a hockey puck if it hit him in the head. He had no idea what the shirt meant; it was just a nifty article of clothing from America.

I'm thinking: pretty freaking cool, this kid is wearing a Red Wings t-shirt. Even more freaking cool was that a donation dropped in a box somewhere in North America reached its intended target, a kid in Africa who needed clothes.

The children held our hands and guided us through a shantytown to a clearing they used as a soccer field. It was a mix of grass and dirt and littered with old tires, which the kids used in inventive ways as toys. The soccer ball was made up of torn pieces of t-shirt sewn tightly around a couple more balled up shirts. Andrew and Monty watched the informal match, played with the children who weren't involved with the soccer game, and listened to them sing. They hugged the kids, they high-fived, they ran around and laughed.

"You go in and you kind of get their bio: they're orphaned by AIDS, running away from abusive families, they're young kids with only other orphans as family," explained Ference. "So if you kind of go in with that and guess what you're going to run into, you'd think, ah, kids fallen on hard times. But what we ran into were sharp kids . . . studying during their vacation time . . . really doing whatever they could to better themselves with whatever available resources they had."

"Another thing that is remarkable is the fact that a lot of them come from impoverished areas and very challenging circumstances," added Montador, "and yet they have hope in their eyes and they're happy and they're enjoying themselves with the things that they do. Their feet are so tough to be running on uneven grass mixed with dirt fields, kicking soccer balls, bumping into each other and getting up with a scrape and just continuing on. I mean, they're tough."

That afternoon we went to another *dogo dogo*, this one on the northern outskirts of the city. A group of eight eighteen-year-old orphan boys in their final year in the program (as the director stated, "they will leave to decide their own fates") put on a musical performance for us. High-energy interpretive dance and singing accompanied drumming on eight drums the teenagers had made themselves from wood and animal hides. The music included anti-war and anti-genocide messages and also focused on the natural beauty of their country. Aside from the artistic element, there was a practical side to the effort. They sold each drum for the equivalent of eight U.S. dollars.

"That's another thing that these schools do in such a great way," Monty said. "There are songs and dances that talk about being free and staying resilient through war and tough times."

It was the first day of a week dominated by smiles. Genuine, beaming African smiles that made us smile so hard we'd start to laugh. They were smiles as sincere as you'll see your entire life: at primary schools in remote villages, during our travels deep in the Serengeti, and while meeting a family in their compound literally in the middle of nowhere.

"Their lives are filled with, compared to North American kids, a lot of hardships," Andrew pointed out. "You would never guess that by their attitudes. They're the first ones to run out in the street and wave to the *mzungu* (white skin) and hold your hand. Just very affectionate and happy and real — nothing pretentious about it."

By day two, our eyes and minds had adjusted to our surroundings. The utter novelty wore off and we gradually acclimated to the social environment and the mission. Monty, the late addition, was all in — a chance to play more games and a chance to shake his booty.

"Music and dance are a part of this culture like no other culture that I've been around, and it's nice because I can dance around with these kids, and though I know I suck, it doesn't matter," Monty said between laughs on day two. "Because it's just having a good time and shaking your hips and expressing yourself that way. Music and dance are just such a great expression of the culture here, and it's awesome to see 100 or 200 kids dancing and singing in unison. It's just quite remarkable."

"Monty took to the trip so naturally, and the kids took to him," Brender remembers. "He and Andrew both looked kids in the eye and stayed with them, they were there every moment. One girl at a school held Monty's hand almost from the time he got out of the van until the moment we left. She was maybe twelve or thirteen, and shy, but she wouldn't leave him. He went with it, happily. Nothing fazed him; he just connected."

At one point, the NHLers were playing soccer on rival teams with kids from two orphanages. Ference's squad won the game on penalty kicks, with Andrew scoring the game winner. He was mobbed by hundreds of children who screamed, jumped up and down, and happily chased him the length of the field.

"It was the biggest goal of my career," Andrew said later while seated next to Montador, rubbing it in. Monty described how his team had taken a dagger to their hearts and how the game was under protest because it wasn't FIFA sanctioned.

Laughter and smiles were, in contrast, always followed by serious contemplation during our daily debriefs.

"How many kids did we high-five today that were HIV positive?" Ference asked, then guessed probably a third of them, maybe half.

"It's just a matter-of-fact thing that people get sick here and children, more often than in other places, have to deal with it and have to bear the brunt of it, sometimes taking over the head of the family at ten years old," stated Montador before drawing a deep breath. "It's just amazing to see how tough they are and to see how they want to enjoy life . . . and they have to deal with situations like this." Monty pursed his lips and seemed to fight back emotion. Our cameraman noticed.

"The most impressive thing I came away with about Steve was that he was so genuine," remembers Gamere. "Just a regular guy who was really appreciative of where he was in life. He was so natural with the kids and able to be cool while also not taking himself so seriously. When we interviewed him by the lake and he got emotional, it

Steve Montador in Tanzania, 2007.

really showed me a lot about who he was and that he really had an understanding for what brought him there."

The lake was Lake Victoria, ruggedly breathtaking and windswept. To start the middle portion of the week, we flew to the city of Mwanza on the lake's southern shore (find and watch the documentary film *Darwin's Nightmare* for a look at life there and a reality check) and stayed at the Hotel Tilapia. It was our stopover before a morning flight on a single-propeller, eight-seater to Mugumu, a town in the Serengeti, the giant region and animal preserve that encompasses northern Tanzania and part of Kenya. Along with the five of us, a young girl about eight years old was on the flight with her younger brother of about five — both of them thrilled to be on the airplane. According to Leila, they didn't know it yet, but they were on their way to a remote village to find out that their mother had died of AIDS.

We crammed as much as humanly possible into the next two and a half days.

Waiting for us at the airstrip were a Canadian woman, an American woman, and a Danish man, all of whom volunteered for Right To Play as project coordinators. The idea was that they would gradually pass along their knowledge and eventually turn over the entire operation to local coaches and mentors. These international volunteers would be our program liaisons for the organized activities and events that unfolded. Our other guides and interpreters for the cultural and lifestyle elements, along with Leila, were locals.

For a portion of day two in the Serengeti, we rode in the back of a pickup truck into the bush where one of our guides, Francis, a member of the Kuria tribe, introduced us to "Mr. Cha-cha," his five wives, and his dozen or so children. Three more of Cha-cha's kids were buried inside the spiked wooden walls of his compound, victims of malaria and diarrhea. Two more lay in hospital.

"You bury family *inside* the home," explained Francis.

The women were absolutely perplexed by our still cameras and, of course, by Gamere's completely alien TV camera. Mr. Cha-cha lived by hunting water buffalo, giraffe, and wildebeest, and by eating the fruits and vegetables that grew in the garden outside the compound walls. They'd eat the pet rabbits if necessary.

Later at a Kuria village, the elders greeted us like royal dignitaries, and we danced fertility dances across from the women while listening to raw, frenzied drumbeats. Soon after, three warriors with spears and machetes, in full face and body paint and battle garb, appeared possessed as they staged dances of aggression that spilled into the crowd. I wasn't really stoked to wait around to find out if I'd been dancing with one of these dudes' girlfriends. I think all of us were relieved to jump back into the pickup for a change of scenery.

We headed back to Mugumu for a massive afternoon event RTP called "The Day of the African Child." Children of all ages literally walked miles to be there to meet these athletes from a faraway land, whom they had never heard of, and to partake in sports and games with them. The boys played soccer while the girls played a form of basketball. Afterwards, Andrew and Monty handed out awards and shook hands with all the children. The females curtsied shyly. Each winner received a rare toy: a tennis ball.

We stayed at the Giraffe Garden Hotel in Mugumu and slept under mosquito nets. Mosquitoes transmit malaria, a disease that kills tens of thousands of Tanzanians each year, and hundreds of thousands more around the world. The five of us were fine either way: we were taking preventative malaria medication, a luxury sadly unavailable to the locals.

These are the facts you're constantly reminded of during your visit. You add each one to the mental pile and move right along.

"As far as what it's done for all of us on this trip," Andrew said, "you know it's going to change your perspective, but . . . it's gonna be hard to see some kids back home complaining about stuff, even myself, complaining about certain things sometimes."

For us, there will never be another run like the one we did at six thirty a.m. with the kids from the Mapinduzi Primary School on our final morning in Mugumu. A run into the Serengeti sunrise.

"Three packs of about ninety kids ran for a half-hour, singing songs and running in unison to a march almost, and it was very powerful because it's something they do every school day," recalled Monty. "Singing with ease, carrying their book bags, wearing shoes that didn't seem to fit, and yet they're just jumping with joy and singing along. Andrew and I were part of the group that led the way . . . it was awesome."

"The music is beautiful and the voices are beautiful," added Andrew. "Running down the road into the horizon of the Serengeti."

Our athlete ambassadors then taught lessons on hockey, what it was and generally how it was played, and demonstrated with mini sticks. After some more music and dancing and a few more group games, we hopped into an SUV to leave.

"One of the toughest things was hopping in the truck and leaving a site," Andrew said. "Just met some kids a few hours earlier and we bonded so quickly."

With the official portion of the Serengeti visit completed, the Right To Play organizers hooked us up with an afternoon safari.

"It was the Discovery Channel come to life," explained Monty. "I didn't know what to expect. I knew we were going on a game drive, but I didn't know we'd have any chance of seeing anything. But when we saw migrating wildebeest

— I heard 1.8 million of them travel seasonally, and we were right in the middle of it — that was pretty amazing."

Hyenas, zebras, elands, smaller antelopes, and a chance to take a leak right into the cradle of civilization. We all stood in a row and did just that behind the over-sized Range Rover, urinating on the Serengeti, looking over our shoulders for lions.

"It's funny, though. You come to Africa and you see wild animals and thousands of wildebeests and it's kind of almost a ho-hum experience," Andrew told our documentary crew afterwards. "It'll be the last thing I talk about when I go home. After all the things we've experienced and the kids that we've met, animals are kind of . . . meh."

That's called staying on message, Andrew. All good and true in some ways, but honestly, the safari was wicked cool, probably a once-in-a-lifetime experience, with our own personal TV camera and expert videographer along for the ride.

The flight back to Mwanza was interesting. Unbeknownst to us, or maybe he was kidding, Monty said he'd been taking flying lessons. He was at the controls during the initial descent and part of the final approach. We landed in Mwanza and returned to the Tilapia for lunch before catching an evening flight back to Dar.

We experienced one more Right To Play activity before flying a puddle-jumper to the island of Zanzibar for rest and relaxation. We explored the marketplace in Stone Town and then hit the beach. It gave us the chance to swim in the Indian Ocean. That night, Patrick and I hopped an overnight flight to Zurich en route home to Boston.

Exhausted, sad to leave, yet very satisfied with our efforts, we took time sitting at the airport to reminisce and reflect.

Endless questions and angles: So many smiles — are the kids miserable when we're not around? Are they unhappy to be poor? Do they know any better? Is less truly more? We'll just have to return some day.

"It's as unique a situation as I've ever been in," Monty had told us. "It's hard to think that I'll ever forget this, and that's why I've been taking a lot of pictures and journaling, just so I can try to digest it all, because it's been an overload of so many great situations, and certainly tough situations where you just feel so much compassion for these kids because they are so bright."

"It makes everything real," Andrew said. "We've read it on paper what they've done and it's on the website, but until you actually see hundreds of kids out at a big sporting event on a field where a junkyard used to exist, that's all Right To Play's work. Right from getting the field in shape to getting the kids mobilized and having an amazing time together. You can't really read about it and fully understand just how happy the kids were to be out there and how amazing it was to watch it. If I go home and try to explain to somebody what it's like . . . you have to really see it and experience it to realize the true power of just getting out and playing."

"It's such a great avenue to reach children," Monty added. "All kids, whether they realize it or not, love to play. So to be able to reach kids with an angle [where] they love to be, it's sending a great message, because there are lots and lots of challenges kids face here, and seeing it first-hand you see tough and challenging situations, and you see great hope and potential for a lot of these kids, because they are so bright and they are so cool and they're doing well in the program."

Based on the desire he expressed to get more involved with Right To Play and other humanitarian and charitable endeavours, one could assume Monty would spend the next few decades of his life piling on life experiences similar to the ones we had in Tanzania. Instead, on February 15, 2015, he was found dead at the age of thirty-five in his home in Mississauga, Ontario.

Police ruled out foul play. While suicide was presumed, his family wouldn't announce a cause of death. Accidental death remains the other possibility; Montador admittedly had experienced drinking problems, drug use, and bouts with depression. Monty's ten-season NHL career essentially ended due to symptoms related to multiple concussions.

Monty had arranged to donate his brain upon his death to the Canadian Sports Concussion Project, headed up by family friend Dr. Charles Tator. The autopsy confirmed the presence of the degenerative brain disease Chronic Traumatic Encephalopathy (CTE), a diagnosis only possible after death and a condition closely associated with blows to the head.

Approximately seventy ex-NHLers have sued the league because of physical damage suffered from playing the game, suggesting that the NHL ignored evidence of long-term effects from concussions. Montador's family joined the lawsuit with the intent of donating any potential proceeds raised from a court decision or settlement toward related medical research.

Their intent is honourable, but I disagree with the

lawsuits. One of the enduring qualities of the sport of hockey is the firehouse mentality — the character, the commitment, and the physicality. Let's face it: it's cultural. It's North American hockey. You've been playing the game your entire life; what part of the physicality and violence caught you completely off guard? Sign a waiver or find something else to do. Become a firefighter. They risk their lives and, in some cases, earn next to nothing. As I wrote in my book *Black and Gold*, former Bruin Derek Sanderson once said, "It's a violent game played by violent people; if you don't like it, watch tennis."

Arguably, the NHL was the last major professional league to go from being a sport that was a business to being a business that is a sport. Not to suggest previous owners weren't in it for the profits, but the sometimes mom and pop simplicity of it all has disappeared. It happened during the reign of Commissioner Gary Bettman (which began in 1993 and continues) in which league revenues have grown exponentially. Along the way, there have been lockouts, expansion fees, and a salary cap. He works for the owners, period. Whether or not some of those executives understand or appreciate hockey's firehouse mentality is irrelevant, it is the familiarity of that concept for the players that makes their lawsuit ironic. It seems to be an after-the-fact money grab in many cases: the NFL players did it in 2013 — why shouldn't we?

I've shared my differences of opinion with the NHL, even when I worked there, but in this case, regardless of whether one likes or dislikes its general disposition over the years, the league shouldn't be held responsible. Steve

Montador and the others knew exactly what they were doing and they absolutely loved doing it. There are sometimes tragic results in any risky walk of life. In Monty's case, to couple all of his health issues and lifestyle choices with hockey head-trauma is overly simplistic and not necessarily chronological.

The NHL created a committee in 1997 to begin studying head injuries, a natural step in the progression. Banning fights or open-ice hits altogether would require an organic effort, a culture change, starting with kids, high school, and college players in the U.S., and junior players in both countries. Rule changes have been introduced and there seems to be a new mentality among players regarding mutual respect and safety. On this track, after a generation or two, it may be a completely new game. I might not watch it, but you'd have a different sport with fewer legalities involved. That's always a bonus.

Here's another idea. Get the NHL Players' Association and the league on the same page as it relates to enforcing dangerous plays and illegal hits to the head, and then *actually* enforce them consistently. Impose severe fines and penalties instead of just saying you're going to impose them. As of early 2018, this also seems to be happening.

Better yet, get the NHLPA to actively track and assist players as they transition from playing into retirement, especially guys who have suffered severe or chronic injuries. Montador's best friend in the game, Daniel Carcillo, retired in 2015 and decided to take matters into his own hands by forming the Chapter 5 Foundation, the number 5 in honor of Monty's jersey number in Chicago. From the website:

> The mission of Chapter 5 is to help athletes discover their new purpose and transition into life after the game. Carcillo was shocked to learn that a single post-retirement phone call from the union, for the most part, made up the extent of transition monitoring. Bye-bye, be tough, move on, just another example of the macho mindset that makes up hockey's code and aforementioned culture.

I was as shocked and as sad as any of his acquaintances upon hearing of Monty's passing. We were involved in a journey that was as unique, consciousness altering, and inspirational as any in our lives. We chatted by phone about once a year the first few years after our trip with Right To Play, and I last saw him at the Leafs practice rink in Toronto, at one of those preseason gatherings organized by Brendan Shanahan to experiment with potential new NHL rules. (Incidentally, banning fighting and violent body checks or cutting the schedule to seventy games so players can actually recover from regular fatigue and pain, weren't on the list. I'm all for the last one.)

Don't blame the game. And the truth is, it's not about why Monty's gone, it's about missing a great guy who had his heart in the right place.

Or, as Monty's dear friend and former teammate Martin Gelinas put it to writer Eric Francis of the *Calgary Sun* in an article four days after Monty's death: "Is it the concussion? I don't know. I don't know what happened and I don't really care. Let's just honour him for who he was and what he did."

Andrew Ference played his last NHL game early in the 2015–16 season for Edmonton. His contract ran through the 2016–17 campaign. He remains active in charitable and humanitarian endeavors, particularly in the area of environmentalism. In 2017, he was named chairman of Alberta Sport Connection, a provincial agency that promotes sports development.

Mark Brender is now the national director for the Canadian office of Partners In Health, an organization that delivers high-quality health care and strengthens health systems for poor and disadvantaged people around the world. See the movie Bending the Arc.

A small portion of Monty in Africa can be seen on YouTube. Search: Monty NHL in Africa 2007

> "The wave of people. The only thing comparable to it was, we started at Battery Park for the Stanley Cup parade . . . You look behind you and you've never seen so many people in your life."

**Nick Kypreos, former New York Ranger
on running the 2013 NYC Marathon**

LEAPS AND BOUNDS

"Never say never" and "never give up": two clichés of inspiration, two we normally hear and go, "Yeah, okay, sounds good." But when you actually apply them, they can light a fire. When the road dead-ends, take a different road.

In 1991, a couple of buddies visiting me in Hawaii decided they were going to go skydiving on the North Shore of Oahu. For $140 or something, you could jump out of an airplane. At that juncture I probably said, "Not a chance, have fun, get the hell away from me." I had no interest in paying to splatter myself on some rocks near the beach.

Yet, three years later, I was jumping out of an airplane for the first time on the North Shore of Oahu.

Here's what changed and here's what was going through my feeble mind. I was doing the jump for television as part of a transition from being a weatherman on TV in Honolulu to being the weekend sports anchor. I was going to *jump through the atmosphere into a new job*. Yes, cheesy and pathetic. Fortunately, that was the concept explanation that the assignment editor generously bought into.

This would be a tandem jump, so instead of making the leap by myself, an experienced skydiver would essentially be riding on my back, making sure one of us remembered to pull the rip cord on the parachute.

In terms of risking my life, I figured if we made it a three-camera shoot, made it real snazzy and gave the skydiving company plenty of publicity, there was no way our chute wouldn't open. If the CBS affiliate guy goes splat, surely they'd be out of business. In other words, please pack the chute *more* better and then double check it a *third* time.

Where nowadays every news story involves a live shot — live from here, live from there — it didn't happen nearly as often in 1994 on Oahu. We had an ancient live truck and stoned dudes operating it (not that there's anything wrong with that). So if I splattered, they'd be doing it the old-fashioned way: racing back to the station with the videotape as fast as possible.

"This is gonna be cool," I tried to say with great conviction to my buddy Roger Fredericks, my golf pro actually, who was stoked to be jumping right after me. He had always wanted to jump out of an airplane but could never find anyone to go with him. Naturally.

Believe it not, by the time the prejump indoctrination is completed, as in, after you've looked at the gear, the packed chute, and have run through the events, you're feeling pretty confident. During the presentation itself, you're awkwardly quiet.

"Mmm hmm, yep, sounds good," I monotoned to the dude who was explaining what he wanted me to do when we first fell out of the plane.

"Oh yeah," he said. "You're a lot bigger than me, dude, so if you don't do this right we're going for one crazy ride."

"Oh really," I said. "Meaniiiiiiing?"

"Meaning you're about a foot taller than me so if you start flailing around and moving your arms or legs, I won't be able to steer us and we won't fall right." A mini nervous breakdown contorted my mind and took me elsewhere. I thought, *He kind of looks like the lead guitarist for REO Speedwagon.*

You actually do think about backing out, but you know you can't. Just when you seriously think about pulling the chute on pulling the chute, a couple of items pop into your head. In my case, don't be a wussy, and remember, ego, you're on TV.

Of the three cameras utilized for our shoot, two of them were actually provided by the skydivers. One was on another skydiver's head who'd be falling right in front of us, another would be on a third skydiver who'd be videotaping our plummet from a distance. The last camera was on the ground.

"Alright, dude. I'm ready."

That changed the moment I walked outside and saw the piece-of-shit airplane.

"Oh, this is gonna be good." Nuts and bolts, maybe some duct tape, definitely some solder. One goes from thinking, *If I don't puss out, I could be jumping out of it* to *Holy shit, thank God we'll be jumping out of it.* The pilot was, like, a twenty-five-year-old dude who was just slightly less stoney.

Meanwhile, Roger was thinking, *I-hope-we-don't-crash-during-take-off* and *will-we-make-it-high-enough?* Okay, good, we were on the same page.

Me first. I said goodbye to Roger and KGMB-TV's Filipino camera dude Sisto Domingo. Great guy. What does it matter if he's Filipino? Because in Hawaii, that's all you need to say about someone to describe them. Men and women of each nationality or ethnic mix have a personality trait that is automatically assigned to that nationality or mix. Call it acceptable, traditional stereotyping with an island twist. One word can dramatically change the charming connotation. *Haole* (white person), local *haole*, mainland *haole*, and fucking *haole* all determine the respective odds of you eventually getting punched.

Sisto was a pretty big dude for a Filipino, had wavy hair, and, like almost all photographers, smoked *da kine*, also known as *pakalolo*. Outside of the weed reference, "da kine" is like "fair dinkum" in the Australian state of Victoria and other places that aren't New South Wales. It's true dat, it's the real deal, it's something genuine.

Up you go. It's noisy as hell on the plane and you're scared shitless.

I don't recall exactly how long it took us to climb 13,000 feet. All I remember is the dude with the '70s moustache who would be riding tandem on my back and hopefully making sure the rip cord got pulled loudly stating, "Here we go."

I scooched over to him by making baby steps on my knees and then turned around very slowly in the cramped space of what was essentially a Honda Civic with wings. Before he leaned against me and clipped the buckles together on the harnesses that would keep us attached while falling, another guy yelled, "DOOR," to alert the pilot, unlatched the handle where the door met the floor, and let it release. It swung up into its new position and the plane lurched slightly. The opening was big enough to allow a human being to fall out.

That is a moment first-time skydivers never forget. Suddenly, the only thing between you and terra firma two and a half miles below is nothing. The powerful sound of the air rushing by the gap provided the perfect audio accompaniment as my heart and stomach drag raced to my throat.

"Whoa, God."

REO Speedwagon on my back started shouting instructions.

The expression on my face could have meant only one of two things: "I'm emceeing a large hockey banquet, and I just pooped my pants," or "I'm just about to jump out of this airplane."

We crept out under the wing as a single human unit. I could finally stretch my legs a little bit, which felt good,

At this point, probably about 10,000 feet
above the North Shore of Oahu.

but we were just outside the aircraft, hanging on to part
of the fuselage.

"Oh. My. God."

Before I knew it, "ONE, TWO, THREE." And we
fell into a summersault. When we first let go, we nose-
dived and did a slow forward flip. At one point, our backs
were to the ground, dude was below me and I was looking
up at the bottom of the airplane as it flew away and we
fell away. Then we continued the flip and ended up face
down. At that point, I remembered the instructions and
threw my arms and hands forward and my legs straight
back, slightly flared. We gained a neutral position and
dude threw out a stabilizer chute by hand. We were 350
pounds, free-falling. For the next thirty-five seconds, I was

just freaking out. Good freaking out. The video shows the skin on our faces flapping. I was making shaka signs with both hands at the camera guy who was four feet away, falling at the same speed as he stared straight back at us. I looked down and looked around. You know you're falling, but you don't really feel like you're falling.

As expected, dude waved his hand in front of my face briskly three times to warn me that he was pulling the rip cord.

"Please open."

It opened. I was bummed at first. The free fall had been spectacular. We watched the second camera guy plummeting in the distance when suddenly his chute opened.

Then we were birds.

Skydiving had never been on my bucket list. In fact, by the time I made a random long-term goal list, it was a couple of years after I had already jumped out of that plane. As we entered this newest millennium, I wrote down six main items that mixed career, personal, and athletic goals. Among the half-dozen: run a marathon. My wife and I had since moved from Hawaii to Idaho, but it was covering the Honolulu Marathon that first gave me the idea.

A marathon was the one thing on the list I thought I had the least chance of accomplishing, and more than once along the way I completely wrote off the possibility. In 2010, I really thought there was no chance in hell. It's four 10Ks plus some. Running 26.2 miles is basically freaking stupid. It's why only 0.5 percent of the American population has run one.

At almost six-foot-seven, 220 to 230 pounds, I'm built for team sports, not running. I played hockey, basketball, soccer, baseball, whatever, but I didn't run for distance. Soccer involved running a lot, but the few times we went long distances in early season school practices, I ran slowly and/or puked.

As an adult, running gradually went from being a simple, tolerable exercise option to something rather enjoyable. It became even more enjoyable when some competition was introduced. My brother Tom had run for years, including in multiple marathons, and we made a habit of getting together once a year for a 10K event. In fact, we annually hand out the Simpson Family Foot Race trophy to the winner of this challenge wherever we are in North America. Unfortunately, or maybe it's fortunately, the kids have taken over, and unless we hold the event and don't tell anyone else, us old guys will never win it again.

Through this gradual acclimation, by 2012, I somehow decided I was ready to run a marathon. I gained entry to New York via a random lottery drawing early in the year. Utterly undecided, I waited until the last day before the invitation acceptance deadline. At that point, it was sign up or lose the chance.

What the hell am I doing? I thought, after pulling the trigger and paying the online entry fee.

Apparently, I had lost my sanity. I began training and ran various distances every other day, minimum of four miles, from May thru October.

Hurricane Sandy then forced the cancellation of the 2012 marathon that had been scheduled for Sunday, November 4. The storm caused seventy-one deaths in the state of New York alone and was the second most expensive hurricane in American history.

I would have been a complete donkey to be upset by the run cancellation. Everyone with any history at all on the East Coast had friends or family whose homes were trashed or destroyed. My pals' houses in New Jersey were under water. I had hung out, worked, and/or lived in the City for more than two decades. It was shocking how long it took NYC Mayor Bloomberg to cancel the race, just two days beforehand. He waited until runners from Europe and the rest of the world had flown in to New York. While I was only ninety minutes away by car or train, true out-of-towners came in and were essentially trapped with very little to do. I found out my hotel was one of hundreds of buildings in Manhattan that didn't even have power until well after the weekend.

In reality, I was somewhat relieved the marathon was cancelled. Had there been a race, I'm not sure I would have survived it. Striving for an unlikely finish, I would have pushed and pushed and pushed, and without the proper salt and nutrient intake, I may have killed myself trying.

Many weeks later, I used my automatic re-entry to sign up again. It was a rebirth, a second chance to get it right. It also meant redoing six months of training.

This time I did my homework. I established a more efficient and effective run calendar, I researched the medical and nutritional side of getting through it, I studied and dreamed of the crazy cool course, and I established a prerun routine. This is what I needed for marathon day:

1. The same model of Asics shoes that I had been running in, but a new pair with somewhere between sixty and one hundred miles on them. It would be my third pair of new runners since May.

2. Three or four little salt packets from McDonald's to restore sodium to my body about every six or seven miles. On long runs, one develops a salt film on their skin, hair, and sometimes on their clothing as the sweat drains everything from the body. It's dangerous not to replenish it.

3. My lucky running sunglasses. It could be foggy or dumping rain, and I'd still wear those "dreamies." I liked the complete anonymity of wearing them, somehow running with privacy.

4. Gu packets. Manufactured in multiple flavours, I'd squeeze these prepackaged little nutritional globs into my mouth probably four to five times intermittently during the marathon.

5. To know how to routinely drink water from a cup and swallow it while running exhausted. It's not easy. Some people have to actually stop. I wasn't stopping.

6. To not take a Gatorade-type drink. Anything but water during strenuous exercise, for whatever reason,

eventually makes me puke, and, for whatever other reasons, the Gu packets don't.

7. Anti-chafing cream. For efforts of ten miles or more, one needs to apply it to all bodily areas that rub against clothing during a run. The inside of the thighs and the nipples are mandatory spots. Sounds like a sadistic, kinky sideshow, but if untreated, one's nipples will scream in pain and bleed from the shirt rubbing up and down against them.

8. Special socks. Yep, running stores sell short socks with extra cushion for just such an event. Runners love them.

9. To decide whether to free ball it or wear boxer briefs. I recall I ended up going commando.

10. No injuries. A wonky knee actually knocked me out of training in May for two weeks. It was still five months before the race, but I thought I was done. Shin splints flared up very briefly on rare occasions, but fortunately were never truly a problem.

11. To remember to carry three or four Tylenol with me. All forms of over-the-counter painkillers are discouraged during a long run as they could mask an injury that requires immediate treatment, but Tylenol is an acetaminophen and doesn't affect your kidneys like ibuprofen. Aspirin and anti-inflammatories are on the no-no list during a marathon. I only planned to take

the Tylenol during the last six miles or so if I knew I was okay and wanted to be more comfortable.

12. Six months of running about every other day. For me it was actually three times a week. Staggered distances over time, eventually with three runs of eighteen miles or longer during the final three months leading up to the race, one of them twenty-two miles. By accomplishing that run a month before the marathon, I knew I could make the twenty-six. Most runs were eight to twelve miles while four or six miles was the default short distance.

13. To run the Toronto half marathon two weeks before New York. (I ran it in 1:59:00.) After that thirteen-mile run, I was officially into the "taper-down," which meant runs of four to six miles max over the final two weeks to rest the body. Toronto was my cleanest, best-ever run, which gave me a great deal of confidence looking a fortnight ahead.

14. A ten- to fifteen-minute stretching routine before and after all runs.

15. Travel arrangements and all the crap that goes with it. Being in all the right places at all the right times. Reality hit when I picked up my race packet and number bib the evening before. "Holy shit, I'm doing this," I said as I walked back to my hotel.

Nick Kypreos, a former National Hockey League player, Stanley Cup winner with the Rangers in 1994, and now a fellow hockey media-type in Toronto, was the only other person I knew of our ilk who was running the race in 2013.

"A lot of stars aligned for me to run in the New York Marathon," Kipper points out. "Rogers Sportsnet was covering the marathon, and they offered a spot for any broadcaster that wanted it, so they brought it to my attention. My first thought was *not a chance*, and then a week later it kind of sunk in that, probably the most opposite thing I'd ever do, running twenty-six miles. Not quite like getting ready for an NHL training camp, but in a lot of ways it brought back a ton of great memories."

Marathon training essentially means vanishing from your family for an extra hour or two or three every couple of days. Add the stretching and the cool down and the shower afterwards, that's another hour. One has no option but to be fully committed. In a way, it's therapeutic. I always ran alone, while Kipper did it differently.

"I trained with some people who had run before; I joined a running group," he said. "I had some personal training, they had me on a pretty good course leading up to the marathon."

Why do it? It's a conquest: a mental and physical battle for someone fit enough to challenge themselves, like a mountain to climb. Kipper did it for the exact same reason I did. I did it for my son; he did it to set the same example for his kids.

"It's an hour, an hour and a half a day where you have to be in the gym doing the various exercises or pounding the pavement or the treadmill. My kids weren't around when I played (NHL hockey), so this was a good opportunity to show them that if you set a goal, you find ways to achieve that goal," Kypreos explained.

I always ran without music and electronics. No watch either. I don't wear one anyway so why wear one running. No belt or fanny pack with little supplies. For longer runs, I'd carry one or two plastic water bottles with me and discard the empties along the way. Otherwise, it was just the road or the sidewalk and me.

This type of exercise is great for thinking, either deep thoughts or random streams of consciousness. Frequent topics: 1) places I'd like to travel that I haven't yet, 2) all the ways the Palestinians are getting screwed over, and 3) a lot of Salma Hayek naked.

There are times during training that you're in actual pain and/or simply bored. During a middle month like August, when I had a week with a ten-miler and a four-miler and then a twelve-miler, I wasn't exactly stoked. But I just kept plugging along and the conditioning results were remarkable. I'd finish a twelve-mile run, even an eighteen-miler later on, and just walk away. No hands on the knees, no drama. The body benefits and adjusts. I was svelte and in great shape. I truly believe anyone with a shitload of determination and without a medical condition can run a marathon.

I actually failed the first time I went eighteen miles in training; I only made it about seventeen. The salt was thick on my forearms, and I was dizzy and lightheaded. Uh oh. Do I have a heart condition? I briefly thought about quitting altogether. Instead, I read up on the salt thing, regrouped on the distance calendar, and planned to make it the next time I tried that distance two weeks later.

On October 13, three weeks out, I ran twenty-two miles. Most who train don't go this far before a marathon, but I needed the distance for reassurance and confidence. I executed the marathon routine as it related to pace and ingesting water and nutrients into my body. When I was done, I knew I could tackle New York. On October 20, I ran the Toronto Half. It remains the best race I ever ran in terms of form and pace. Never deviated, basically ran nine-minute miles.

After two weeks of a very pleasant taper-down, it was time for New York.

Marathon morning, I left my hotel about ten blocks from the finish line and began the most bizarre round trip I'd ever make. Instead of hopping on the subway at Fifty-First Street, I walked eleven blocks to Grand Central, which allowed me to breathe a little and see the streets before the madness, and hopped on the 4 or 6 train downtown. I popped up at the last stop in Manhattan and wandered over to Battery Park and the Staten Island Ferry Terminal. They herded us aboard. The organization of the transportation was remarkable. Some runners took buses from the city, others private transportation. I signed up for the boat because, for me, it was the only way to go; it epitomized New York. You leave the downtown end of Manhattan, pass the Statue of Liberty on the way through the harbour, and end up at the north end of Staten Island.

I was near the back of the herd, but I managed to walk along the port side of the ship to an open spot on the floor near the front of the boat. I sat on the deck against a wall, with my legs stretched out. There was a quiet, somewhat nervous pall. People who knew what they were getting into, veteran marathoners, carried a certain confidence, but I sensed there were plenty of other first-timers like me. One girl expressed doubt about finishing the race to her friend.

She won't be finishing the race, I thought. Positive thinking is at a premium.

The boat pulled up, a ramp was lowered, and I ended up being the first person leaving the port side. Cool.

But that brief emotional boost was squashed the second I walked through the busy terminal and stepped outside. A long line of marathoners wound up the terminal driveway to the road, turned right along a fence, and down along a hill to where buses by the dozens were stopping to pick up runners. Thank God I didn't have to take a leak.

Twenty-five minutes later and about halfway through the line: "Oh my God. I have to piss." Don't think about it; don't think about it — hop, hop, hop. Warm bus, warm bus, warm bus, *please.*

About that same time, the professional runners were starting the marathon at the base of the Verrazano Bridge. After the elite men left at 9:40, the rest of us would depart in waves by the thousands. First we had to get there. I squirmed my way on board a bus. I sat halfway back next to a really cool middle-aged black guy from Detroit who was running his fourth or fifth marathon. We reminisced about Tiger Stadium.

It seemed like only about a ten-minute trip. I unloaded, walked through and around cops and more cops, hit the Porta-Potty, and then wound my way to my colour-coded corral area. I was in the green corral, the only one on the south side of the bridge, and my start time was 10:40 a.m., also known as the third wave. Each runner had an assigned start time and a corral and shared, with thousands of others, potties, snacks, drinks, and grassy areas for stretching.

I had a banana, a little bit of water, half a cup of coffee, and peed again. Twenty minutes from our start time, I began the greatest stretch of my life, singularly focused, methodical, perfect. I was getting anxious. Then I took a final small leak. I wanted to be completely empty. I had no intention of stopping for any reason during the marathon, especially to take a whiz.

After a few more minutes of apprehensively standing around, our wave regrouped en mass on the base of the bridge, and my marathon began with a mixture of relief, disbelief, and fascination. I suddenly found myself running in a herd of humanity up and over the Verrazano Bridge on the way to Brooklyn. It's actually a decent climb. The adrenaline, the people, the pace, carries you along with a tempered joy.

The Boston Marathon in the spring of 2013 had been bombed. The New York City Marathon seven months later had security like you wouldn't believe. One indelible image remains with me. Halfway across the bridge, just before the crest, looking left, an NYPD helicopter hovered perfectly still just dozens of feet away from us, with the city harbour and skyline as the backdrop. The Statue of Liberty, the Hudson River stretching away, downtown, the East River, and Brooklyn, our next destination.

Kypreos recalls it. "I mean I lived in New York and won a Stanley Cup there, but I've never seen New York quite like that before, that was one of the coolest things I've ever done."

The crowds gradually pick up as you leave the bridge and work your way into Brooklyn. By the time you hit a ridiculously long trip up Fourth Avenue, there are tens of thousands of people lined along the sides of the route. There's garage bands, an opera singer, reggae, a jazz quartet, set up blocks apart, and a cop on every corner on both sides of the street all the way through. I ran along the left edge by the median and fist bumped a bunch of policemen on my way by.

"You'd think at some point over twenty-six miles that the crowd would waver a little bit," Kipper adds, "but Brooklyn, with their signs, and just, they were relentless in their cheering, they never wavered. They were always pushing you. They were as involved as the runners, the people watching. That's incredible. You try to describe it to people but you have to experience it."

The crowd encourages you through most of Brooklyn. You finally turn right onto a lovely tree-lined street that takes you east about twenty or so blocks before you turn back north towards Queens. The crowds wane through Park Slope with just the occasional Hasidic Jew or two wandering along on either side. Through Williamsburg the crowds pick back up as you meander towards the Pulaski Bridge that takes you over the Newtown Creek and, finally, into the next borough. The relatively short trip through a little slice of Queens is pleasant knowing that the Queensboro Bridge isn't far off. The adrenaline kicks in again as tens of thousands more supporters await you in Gotham.

It's at this point every marathoner must be concerned about what's called "hitting the wall." The wall is the psychological barrier that screams, "You're done, you can't do this anymore, where the hell do you think you're going?!"

It can actually happen on any long run as your brain starts to consider reaching the finish.

"Oh, yeah, absolutely, absolutely," remembers Kypreos. "I was maybe about sixteen or seventeen miles in and that's when I was just like . . . what am I doing?"

Coming off the bridge, mile sixteen is the start of the long stretch up First Avenue in Manhattan, a pretty typical place for the wall. About a mile into this stint, I felt my acute mental anguish. I dragged ass for four miles until I hit the Willis Avenue Bridge to the Bronx. Thank God for the bagpiper waiting at the other end of the bridge. I first heard him, then I saw him, then I passed him, and at that point I knew I was good to go the distance. Not sure if it was some emotional connection with my Scottish heritage or the fact that the route through the Bronx offered short stints of road, with quick turns, and no long stretches. We weaved back and forth and then into Manhattan via the Madison Avenue Bridge.

Way uptown on Fifth Avenue, I left any thought of quitting behind as I popped a Tylenol, eventually taking three of them over the final five miles. My legs were hurting, but I knew I would finish. Masking an injury? Oh well, at that point I didn't give a shit. Comfort first.

"You just try to envision finishing it," adds Kipper. "Getting to Central Park was really tough for me; it was actually easier once I got into Central Park. That's when I felt like there was light at the end of the tunnel. Prior to that there was a short stint of three or four miles to get to Central Park where I really battled."

I felt a similar calm. I had run the Central Park loop dozens of times, meaning the last four miles of the marathon were alongside and inside my comfort zone, a familiar friend. We actually exited the south end of park onto Fifty-Ninth Street on the east side near the Plaza Hotel, ran the width of the park along its base before re-entering at Columbus Circle. The satisfaction of running that last short bit on the west side, envisioned so many times before, is difficult to describe. Surreal, still unbelievable — a mountain climbed.

Never say never and never give up.

I finished the marathon in four hours and forty-four minutes. Kypreos is a wanker simply because he finished it in 4:40. That's right, four minutes faster. By the way, we never actually saw each other; we were running in different waves. Ultimately, the times meant nothing. We ran the whole way and we finished. There is little chance either one of us will ever run another one.

Roger Fredericks went on to become one of the world's leading golf instructors, utilizing his unique focus on flexibility, fitness, and video analysis. Based in So-Cal, he's helped the likes of Arnold Palmer, Jack Nicklaus, and a number of celebrity golfers.

Meanwhile, the simplest thing on my long-term goal list was to slam dunk a basketball at age thirty-five and forty. I have since done it at forty-five and fifty, with fifty-five still in the plans. There is only one thing I have not yet accomplished on that list. What's referred to in Hawaii in the local Pidgin language as bachi *prevents me from revealing and jinxing it.*

The actual skydive on YouTube: Simmer Hawaii Skydive

"Yeah, well, don't get too worked up about all this radio stuff . . . I thought you wanted to be a veterinarian."

———

**Marge Simpson (my mom),
January 1980**

THE GROWLING

If the Detroit Pistons hadn't stunk, I probably wouldn't have been given the opportunity to cover them as a teenager.

Eric Forest, Ric Blackwell, and I worked together as students at WBFH-FM, a high-school radio station in Bloomfield Hills, Michigan, a white-collar, middle-class to affluent area about twenty-five minutes north of downtown Detroit and about twenty minutes from the Pistons' former home, the Pontiac Silverdome.

The experience started in tenth grade with Fundamentals of Radio Broadcasting class, also known among its graduates, and to the teacher, Pete Bowers, as "fun with mentals." It was here we learned to disc jockey, to write copy, and put together two-minute news reports. We also learned the necessary FCC rules and regulations to get our operators' licenses. Back then, you needed a license to be a DJ. This meant taking a government test, which was remedial once you had completed the fundamentals.

Eric was first to contact Bill Kreifeldt, then–public relations director for the last-place Pistons. "Mr. Kreifeldt," as we will refer to him eternally, was very open to the idea of allowing young students the opportunity to be exposed to the world of professional media. I'm sure he was this generous with novices like us only because the Pistons were absolutely lousy. Our local NBA basketball team was in the midst of the 1979–80 season, which would see them finish with a franchise-record worst of sixteen wins and sixty-six losses. Media coverage for the club was apathetic at best. Tickets and media passes were easy to come by. Of course, we didn't mind being in the right place at the right time.

On January 13, 1980, I was riding in Eric's Chevrolet Chevette, a glorified golf cart, with a bit of an upset stomach. Not only did Eric's erratic driving make me nervous, but I had only about ten minutes to get my thoughts together before arriving at the dome. The Pistons hosted the Chicago Bulls. The game meant little in the standings, but it meant everything to me: my first as a reporter. I was excited as I clutched my little brown sports bag with the white stripe over the top. In it, an oversized cassette recorder, a handy little microphone, two pens, and a note pad.

Eric parked the Chevette in the vast concrete pasture

of the parking lot. We hopped out, made our way to the east gate, down the huge outdoor funnel of an entry area, and into the revolving doors.

"Dubbayu-bee-ef-aich," Eric spat out into the slot at the will-call window. Eric had kind of a lispy speech impediment. The lady behind the plastic window shuffled some tiny envelopes and then slid one towards Eric.

"Thanks." Eric turned and nervously tried to open the end of the envelope with his thumb. His hands were shaking as he turned the envelope in his hands, trying to get his finger under the fold. His chronic nervousness was making me anxious.

"Let me see," I urged.

"I got it!" Eric tore the envelope open and pulled out two little square white cards. On the front was the Pistons emblem, beneath it a line with the date on it, and below that another line with "Chicago" stamped on it. The top of the card had a hole in it with a little white string tied through the opening.

I snagged one of the cards from Eric and attached the string to one of the belt loops on the front of my pants. We proceeded down a stairway leading through the huge main lower section of blue seats, stepping down about fifty or sixty rows from the top of the section all the way to court level. The further we descended, the bigger the Silverdome seemed to get.

It opened in 1976–77 as the home of the NFL's Detroit Lions. The area at ground level that made up the football field was cut in half by a nine-storey blue curtain that hung along the fifty-yard line. On our side of the curtain, a hardwood basketball floor extended out from the corner of the end zone. People sat in the football stadium seats on one side and end of the court, while temporary grand-stands were rolled in and set up along the other side and far end of the court. I can't seem to recall why the Pistons moved from downtown Detroit, from the acoustically perfect Cobo Arena, to play basketball inside a football stadium. Oh, yeah, that's right, people had been getting stabbed a lot in downtown Detroit.

The featured high-school game, which served as the warm-up event before the Pistons game, was wrapping up. In twenty minutes or so, the NBAers would take to the court for their pregame "shoot-around," their idea of loosening up.

The little white card dangling above my groin worked magic. We slid past the guards at the bottom of the steps with a "How ya doin'?" and made our way along the end of the court. A gradual left turn brought us face to face with the yawning mouth of the Silverdome's tunnel.

The *tunnel*.

I had stared at it dozens of times at NFL games in the past, wondering where it led and what was inside. It was the tunnel Billy Sims, Al "Bubba" Baker, and Gary Danielson had disappeared into time after time, often during or after a loss.

Now *I* was making the walk into the echoing dimness.

The concrete sloped up from under one big hydraulic door, and forty yards or so further, there was an even bigger door at the back of the tunnel. The floor was sloped enough that you could feel a slight effort in your legs. Although dumbfounded as I walked, I managed to notice the Pistons locker room door off to my left about fifteen yards up. The door was painted blue, with a big red-and-white Pistons emblem painted in the middle. We continued past.

Fifteen yards from the end of the tunnel, I wondered where we were going. Straight ahead of us stood the aforementioned second huge door, which was big enough to allow for a tractor trailer, or an elephant, or both at the same time. To its left, a regular walk-in door was guarded by a grumpy-looking rent-a-cop.

"Hey?" He paused. "Where are your passes?"

Who's this dipshit? I thought, glancing down at the card hanging from my belt loop.

"Umm, right here," Eric and I said together, nervous with inexperience.

"Sign in," the guard ordered, turning the sheet in a binder towards us. Eric's hands shook as he scribbled. As he was doing that, I noticed a well-lit corridor running off to our left, next to the security guard and his little podium. Eric handed me the pen, and I scribbled my name and WBFH. The gruff, cranky-looking guard cracked a grin. I waited as if something else was supposed to happen. An awkward moment later, Eric turned and led me into the light.

A closed double door, which turned out to be the entrance to the visitors locker room, stood in front of us, but, before reaching it, we took a left turn down a shorter well-lit corridor. Then we took a right, where the press room opened up in front of us.

The room was quite simple. White concrete walls surrounded us, steel-framed cage lockers ran along the left side, and seven or eight rows of long dining tables and chairs crossed in front of us and blocked our way to the back of the room. It was clean, but it smelled like chicken. Dinner trays lined the longest table of them all, which ran half the length of the room on the right, perpendicular to the others. At one end of this long table, paper plates and napkins; at the other, little brownies, each square placed on its own individual mini dessert plate. The middle of the table held trays full of chicken, potatoes, rice, and salad.

Behind the edibles stood two women dressed in Elias Brothers waitress outfits — Elias Brothers being the local equivalent of Big Boy Restaurant. One woman was slim and attractive; the other, short, stout, and not so attractive. To me, this was glamour.

So I'm thinking, *Let me get this straight. We get a free pass to the game, we come in here for a free meal served by a hot babe and her chubby friend, and then I get to interview basketball players?*

We grabbed our plates and made our way along the table. The babe picked out a couple of chicken breasts and set them on my plate. We found a table with no one at it and sat down. Now what?

"Eat," Eric said as if hearing my thoughts. "I'll grab the game notes."

Eric went to a locker and grabbed us a glossy program and a small stack of white statistics sheets. He dropped the packet in front of me. Glancing through the notes, I was startled and impressed. There were updates on every player, including their efforts from the last game, season stats, quirks, injuries, and personal notes. There was also a section about the rest of the NBA and more in-depth items about the Bulls, the Pistons' opponent.

So that's how sportscasters know all of that stuff: someone hands it to them.

Scanning the room, I recognized only a couple of people. I'd seen Charlie Vincent's little picture above his column in the *Detroit Free Press*. Nice guy.

After dinner, Eric led the way out of the press room, down the tunnel, and out towards the court. The press table courtside was full. We still sat very close to the action, in a media spill-over section just to the left of the Pistons bench behind the baseline. Had it been a football game, we'd have been sitting in the back corner of the end zone. The play was intense. We could see the sweat fly and hear the contact, the moans, the language, and the trash talking.

At the end of the half, it was time to head back up the tunnel to grab a soda pop. After a little schmoozing in the middle of the tunnel, mostly just with Eric, we headed back out carrying our little clear plastic drink cups.

I always savoured that walk, particularly before and after the game when the path to the court was roped off. Fans stood along the sides craning their neck, waiting for players to walk past. At one point or another, they'd get me instead. I'd walk by making sure not to stumble. Just before we media types reached the playing surface, we'd slip under the rope and walk down the aisle at the end of the court to take our seats. A few — including me, once I gathered the confidence — would walk right onto the court, along the baseline, and then to our seats. After the games, it was even more fun because, if you hustled, you could catch the players leaving the court and join them as they strutted back into the tunnel. This opened the opportunity for informal rap before the players could reach the locker room. Sometimes I'd just walk next to them or behind them and marvel at their enormous size. It was literally like strolling among trees: huge men — the forwards averaging six-foot-eight, six-foot-nine, 230 pounds — grumbling along, sweating, and, sometimes, cussing.

As the second half began that first night, I had already begun thinking nervously about the post-game. Soon I would be talking to these guys. The statistician's runner, a relatively short, thin guy with early Beatles hair and a moustache, dropped off a copy of the first-half stats to each of us, and I began to study the sheet. I was bent on being prepared. The second half seemed to last an eternity, especially the last three or four minutes. The teams must have called six timeouts. Finally, the horn sounded. The Pistons had lost *again*, and it was time to make my interviewing debut. We walked hurriedly back to the press room to grab our tape recorders.

"I'll grab the Pishtons, you grab the Bulls," Eric slurred as he lumbered off awkwardly at his top speed.

"Great."

The hallway that led from the tunnel to the press room branched off and turned towards the visitors locker room as well. I made my way in that direction and steered toward what looked like a group of reporters in front of the locker room door. I assumed they were waiting to go in.

I stopped behind the group and nervously began walking in small circles. Looking up, looking down, looking this way and that, I tried to look preoccupied.

"When do they let us in?" I asked the nearest guy.

"Shhhh!" was his quick response.

"What are you doing?" another reporter asked me, leaning backwards.

I had no idea, frankly. But I suddenly realized these reporters were already busy. Chicago head coach Jerry Sloan was addressing the media and answering questions in front of the closed door. I fumbled for my microphone and hit Record and Pause on my tape recorder. I then slid around the coach's left side and put my mic under his face.

I tried to listen intently but was simply too caught up in the scene. Shortly, one by one, the reporters began to drop off. They had heard all they needed to hear and began to move on. A few went through the door behind the coach and into the Bulls dressing room. I stayed until just three other reporters were left. Then I bolted, to avoid having an accidental one-on-one situation with Jerry Sloan. I wasn't ready for that, and I had nothing to ask.

I pulled open the locker room door and almost collided head-on with a fast-moving trainer who was cruising out in a hurry. I spun around and tried to gather my senses. The visitors locker room was like a high-school locker room, with simple cage lockers and tile flooring. However, unlike *my* high-school locker room, the players here were mostly big, black, and naked. I could hear the showers through an opening at the far end of the room. Players came in and out carrying or wearing towels. Media types clustered around in small groups. The players calmly answered questions as they put on their clothes or packed small gym bags or toiletry bags.

I thought I recognized Reggie Theus. Then I thought

I recognized David Greenwood. A group of reporters stooped over him.

"Yeah, that's David Greenwood," I said under my breath. *I'll go join them*, I thought.

In a nervous fog, I took about two steps and tripped. I stumbled forward and barely held on to my tape recorder. Still attached, the microphone and its cord slipped out of my hand and hit the floor. Just as I gathered myself, I stumbled a second time. I reached out and touched the floor with my left hand to stop a headfirst plunge.

In an instant, I reeled the cord in hand over hand, cradled my equipment, gathered my senses, and stood upright. Immediately, I looked down to my right and realized what had happened.

I had tripped over Artis Gilmore. Actually, I kicked him *as* I tripped over him. Twice.

Gilmore growled at me.

Yes, Artis Gilmore, maybe the biggest, meanest, most physical centre in the NBA in his era, growled at me. He was seven-foot-two and weighed 265 pounds; he sported a big afro, a Fu Manchu moustache-and-beard combo that connected to his sideburns. He was sitting on the floor with his back against a locker, legs fully extended, with large ice packs strapped to both knees. He was huge, nasty looking, and in pain. His legs seemed to stretch halfway across the room.

Meanwhile, I was in full Barney-Fife-who-just-saw-a-ghost mode.

"Hubbada, hubbada, hub-bah, bah, bah." It was the only time in my life I actually swallowed my voice. I thought he was going to eat me, or at least just crush my

"Simmer" at age seventeen, sitting in the
Andover High School radio station.

skull. I squeaked out a "sorry." He stared at me for a few
more excruciating seconds and then looked back down
at his knees and adjusted his legs. Now his knees *and* his
ankles hurt.

Moments later, the stress of the situation rushed
me. I sort of blacked out on my feet. I was standing in a
room holding a tape recorder and microphone, mentally
spinning in circles. I had no support. It was me, a fifteen-
year-old suburban white boy, the media, and a dozen professional athletes.

What seemed like an eternity probably lasted only
five seconds. That's when I realized that only Artis and
I had been involved in the incident. As preoccupied as
I was with my awkwardness, no one else was paying the
slightest bit of attention. At least that's how it seemed.

My next move — what else — interview Artis. I cautiously moved over to him and leaned over. "Can I ask you something?"

He grunted, "Yeah." I asked him two or three questions, he gave me relatively brief answers, and I wished him good luck. I then carefully stepped around Artis and made a beeline for the locker room door.

I stumbled out into the corridor and decided to take a quick little breather in the press room. I wandered in, moved my little brown bag out of the way, and sat down in a cage locker for a moment. That's when I made a startling discovery.

The Jerry Sloan and Artis Gilmore comments were lost forever. I never recorded them. I never released the pause button.

After a couple of deep breaths, I moved on. I made my way back into the tunnel and down towards the Pistons locker room. When I took a right into the recessed entry way, the door was closed.

Obviously, everyone who needed or wanted to go in had done so. At this point, I wasn't positive that I had free rein, nor did I have the confidence to wander in, despite the "backstage pass" that dangled above my crotch. After an uncomfortable moment, a security guard stepped over and saved me. It was the same guy who sat just behind the Pistons bench and kept an eye on the crowd during the games.

"What's up?" he smiled and asked.

"Just hangin' out for a moment," I said, shuffling awkwardly. "I was just in the Bulls locker room and . . ."

"You can go in. It's wide open now," he said, gesturing to the door.

"Yeah, thanks." I paused for a moment as if to suggest I knew that already and then made a move for the locker room.

For the second time that evening, just as I reached a door, someone else came rushing through it. This time, instead of a Bulls trainer, it was a Pistons public relations assistant. The door crunched into my shoulder with a dull thud and then continued into my hand and my plastic tape recorder.

As I grunted, more startled than pained, the tape recorder fell three feet to the concrete below.

Oh no, I thought, as I watched it fall in what seemed like slow motion. Of course, it didn't land flat on its back or on its side; it hit the ground on an angle, right on the corner by the battery compartment.

Crack! The compartment lid popped off and four C-sized batteries came bouncing out. Two stayed close, one did three flips toward the middle of the tunnel, and the last one rolled downhill in a hurry. The security guard stopped the bouncing battery with his foot. The other renegade picked up speed as it left the locker room entryway, took a right-hand turn, and headed down the tunnel towards the big door. The big door was open. If the battery kept its momentum, it could roll twenty yards to the end of the courtside stands.

Meanwhile, the PR guy who had rocked my world continued on his way up the tunnel after a brief "sorry."

After scooping up the recorder, the compartment lid,

and the batteries nearby, the pursuit began. The security guard handed me battery number three as I bent over to keep an eye on the runaway. A few players' friends and relatives milling around inside the tunnel chuckled. As I cradled what I had collected, I took a step out into the tunnel and noticed the runaway battery turning a left partway down the slope. After a fifteen-yard roll, it came to rest at the feet of four very well-dressed African-American women, after caroming off one of their shoes. They didn't notice the Rayovac and continued chatting.

"Excuse me," I said, red-faced as I reached down between the collection of legs.

"No, excuse *me*, honey," one said with a smile as I picked up the bastard battery. The group laughed together.

Never to this point in my life, despite some pretty solid efforts, had I ever felt like such a dork. I put the tape recorder back together and walked past the security guard into the Pistons locker room.

"Watch out," he said smiling.

Relief replaced apprehension as I finally entered.

What a difference being the home team makes. The visitors not only had to travel and play in front of a hostile crowd, but their locker room was a joke compared to the home team's. While the visitors made do with simple basics, the Pistons locker room was beyond comfortable, with a carpeted hallway beginning just inside the door. As I walked ahead, I passed a coach's room on the right and then a training room. Longtime trainer Mike Abdenour was rubbing the legs of a player who was laid out on a table. The media could see what went on in there, who was getting taped or iced, but like in the other major sports, the training area was definitely off limits. After another ten steps, I stood in the players' locker area. It opened to the right: twelve tall lockers, with name plaques above and plush carpet below. Music thumped from speakers in the ceiling. Every Pistons interview would have accompanying music in the background. Bump, thump, bump.

The Pistons appeared dejected after the loss. A few sat on stools and answered questions, a few dressed, while a couple of stragglers wandered out of a door from the showers. This night, twelve players and maybe eight members of the press, including Eric, half-filled the room. Again, the lowly Pistons weren't exactly Detroit's number-one draw. Their season included separate losing streaks of seven, eight, thirteen, and fourteen games. The last streak closed out the season, finishing a larger, miserable run that saw them lose thirty-one of their last thirty-four games. They finished sixteen and sixty-six. And you wondered why high-school kids were getting press passes.

I spotted Eric interviewing John Long, a local favourite who played college ball at the University of Detroit, as did his Pistons teammates Terry Duerod and Terry Tyler.

Eric shifted his weight a lot, and his extended microphone hand shook. Long appeared pained, and he finished his answers quickly. Eric thanked him, shut off his recorder, turned, saw me, smiled, and bobbed his way over.

"Howsh it goin'?" he slobbered.

"Just fabulous, how about you?"

"Good." A big smile came across Eric's face as he brought his head close to mine. "Pwetty cool, huh? Huh? Look at dis." Eric gestured to the rest of the room. "The NBA man, you know? Pwetty cool?"

"Definitely," I answered. Eric was bugging me, but he was right. It *was* pretty cool. To this point, despite some moments of extreme angst, it was a (potentially) once-in-a-lifetime experience. I scanned the room, took it all in, and then suggested scramming. "Are you done, wrapped up?"

"Hmm, yeah. Let's go," he answered.

I followed Eric to the locker room door.

"So, when's our next game?" I asked hopefully on the way out.

Eric smiled and kept on walking.

Eric Forest is a customer care manager for American Airlines at JFK. He's bilingual, French and English, and his "impediment" when we were in high school was actually just an accent. If only the rest of us knew how fortunate he was to fluently speak two languages, but we were teenagers, pretty much jock brains, and it was 1980.

> "Gambling is a disease of
> barbarians superficially civilized."

**Late English author
Dean Inge**

THE GAMBLER

I paid my bookie Lon about $110,000 in losses over a ten-year period. In year eleven, when I went up eight grand, he never paid me. He still hasn't. That's when I quit. It was 2006.

During that decade, I did what many who gamble on sports do — let's face it, there's plenty of us; illegal sports betting in the United States has been estimated to do hundreds of billions of dollars in annual business — I screamed at football officials on the television; I constantly went back and forth to my computer or phone checking scores, whether I was out to dinner, walking the dog, or home watching TV; and I rearranged my financial life so that I could pay off my losses.

Annually flushing ten grand down the toilet takes its toll, especially during a period when I was making only between forty and 110K a year. Of course, with all the other costs of life — house, car, wife, kid, taxes — it didn't make a whole lot of sense. But I was compulsive.

I wouldn't refer to myself as an addict. I could go periods of time without making bets, skip parts of seasons, but being what my recent ex-girlfriend refers to as a lifelong jock comes with its disadvantages. We often hear about the dilemma professional athletes go through when they have to retire from their game — the struggle to adjust to a different life. Well, what about amateur athletes, those of us who played soccer, hockey, baseball, and/or pick-up basketball their whole lives and are no less mentally competitive than any pro athlete? One part of the urge to gamble is an extension of the competition, the need to win. The rest was the adrenaline rush of actually winning and, of course, the thought of cashing in.

The losing cost me a couple of investments and a ton of unnecessary stress. The winning is what galled me to quit. The scumbag I had paid faithfully all those years decided in the end, once the amount got a bit too large, that he wasn't going to honour his commitment back. More accurately, he kept my winnings from the Costa Rican service he worked with for himself. Apparently, he was spending my money to bet on the horses in San Diego.

See, if I lost, I'd send him the money, he'd take his cut, and then send the rest to the big boys offshore. If I won, he was supposed to forward the money to me. He took his cut all those years, and when it came time to pass along a significant win, he pocketed it instead. He was the go-between; the actual bets were made on an 800-number. Many of you know exactly what I'm talking about. Obviously, the percentages and arrangements between a bookie and a service can vary.

I quit while I worked covering the Boston Bruins on TV. In my virtuous good-sportsmanship mind, I refused to bet on any Bruins game; I felt it wouldn't be sporting. But I did bet on NHL games, and I killed it. Once I decided to bet on hockey, I was nailing three-team or four-team parlays on an every-other-day or every-third-day basis. It was ridiculous. And at the end, I was throwing down and often making $200 to $400 on my straight-ups.

(In a parlay, instead of making just a straight up bet, as in Detroit over Chicago, you make three, four, or more picks all on one bet, and you have to get them all correct. Being that it's more difficult to predict multiple outcomes instead of just one, your odds and your payout go up accordingly. So instead of winning twenty bucks on twenty bucks in a straight up bet, in a three-team parlay I'd risk twenty dollars to win a six-to-one return, as in $120. It's bad for the bookie when a very confident gambler starts routinely winning ten-to-one four-team parlays when they're betting $100 a click.)

By the way, a gambler who wagers big money, thousands and tens of thousands of dollars, and mostly loses, is known as "a whale." Bookies adore them and have no problem accepting their money, life savings or not. But then again, that applies to losers from any socio-economic status, bookies and casinos are very, very, happy to take your money.

When I didn't get paid for those winnings, I finally said enough was enough. I haven't placed a bet on any kind of game since. I was so disgusted, so disinterested in re-entering the "market" with another potential scumbag, I bowed out completely. No counselling, no group therapy, no hesitation — I just quit cold turkey. I logically and emotionally realized, like my conscious decision to quit wasting my time watching television for the most part, that there were many more productive and enlightening ways to spend my time.

This doesn't make me special. I'm no different or better off than my acquaintances and friends who *did* require some outside help. We're all victims. Of what, ultimately, I don't know. I will say this: the fact that TV sports networks and radio talk shows routinely tout their picks, the betting lines, and everything that goes with it, isn't helping. I had one good friend drink himself to death because of his gambling losses.

It appalls me that the province of Ontario sponsors Pro-line, which allows for gambling on pro sports, including hockey. When I watched James van Riemsdyk of the Toronto Maple Leafs fire a shot on goal one night at the Air Canada Centre but then didn't ever see the shot registered, I thought, *I wonder if JVR's or the team's shots-on-goal total is a gimmick bet on Pro-line?* Did the off-ice official take the under? Pro-line is a bad idea on a lot of levels, especially for the young hockey fans of Ontario.

In my situation, it didn't help that I was a sportscaster.

Sportscasters are privy to a lot of facts and numbers and are surrounded by other so-called experts. Television, radio, and newspaper sports guys, it would be safe to say, gamble in much higher numbers per capita than the general public. Trust me when I tell you that portions of major sports network newsrooms could just as easily be referred to as "gambling dens."

It starts out harmlessly enough. I was making ten or twenty dollar bets on college football games with an occasional two-team parlay (returns about two and a half to one odds) and two-team teasers. In football, teasers allow you to add six points to any line in either direction on two different selections, and you have to get both predictions correct to win. It's a straight up bet financially — bet twenty bucks to win twenty bucks. But let's say the line on the Green Bay–Detroit game was Packers minus five. Meaning if you bet on the Packers straight up, they would have to beat the Lions by more than five points for you to win the bet. In a teaser, instead of betting twenty bucks for Green Bay to beat Detroit by five, I could give myself six points, making the bet Detroit minus one. I'd take Green Bay. I'd then have to include a second similar selection and get that correct as well. Maybe if the Patriots were a four-point favourite over the Jets, I'd make it New England by ten, and take the Jets plus the points. So the Jets could lose, but they'd have to lose by less than ten. If I got both halves of the teaser correct, I'd win the bet. It's called a gimmick.

Gimmicks make it more fun. Gamblers like it; bookies love it. Bookies also count on you gradually betting more and more as time goes by.

In 1994, I might have been betting twenty to fifty

dollars a game. In 2004, I was betting $100 to $400 a game. Not insane, but getting there.

I also sought outside advice. Not to quit, but to win. For a few football seasons, I actually subscribed to a pick newsletter and phone service run by Phil Steele. Its concept was simple: you pay for him to pick winners, which he provided via newsletter and on subscription phone recordings. He's a big business with a very large willing customer base. By the end of our three- or four-year business relationship, I was referring to him as Phil "Steal." After the third consecutive exclusive ultimate "5-star pick" failed during one college football season, whereafter I had to listen to Phil grimly and remorsefully apologize for letting us down on his voice-recorded follow-up message, I quit him. He can brag all he wants about his winning percentages and being a genius — the dude definitely does massive research — but a loss is a loss, and the gambler is ultimately the one paying for it while also paying Phil for his pick service. No hard feelings, though; I was a willing customer.

It's crazy that I remember gambling moments. Early in my "career," sitting in a sports bar in Hawaii, I'm one out away from winning a three-team parlay worth about $225. That was a rare large amount of dough at that early stage of my efforts. I was betting on baseball playoff games and had nailed the first two parts of the bet. It was October 4, 1995. The Colorado Rockies led the Atlanta Braves 4–3 in the ninth inning of Game Two of the National League Divisional series. All I needed was Rockies second baseman Eric Young, after fielding a routine grounder, to throw the ball to first base for the final out of the game. That was it: Rockies win, I win.

At Game Two of the 1998 Stanley Cup Final with Steve Burchill, Mike Nowland, and Mike's father-in-law John Hydar. I was wagering in those days, but not on hockey.

Instead, Young threw the ball away for his second error of the game, the Braves went on to score four runs in the inning and win the game 7–4. It took a while to get over that one — and to not hate Eric Young.

August 30, 2002. I'm watching the Tulsa Golden Hurricanes versus Oklahoma Sooners game on ESPN. The Sooners were ranked number-one in the country in college football. Tulsa ends up losing 37–0. No surprise there. But the line must have been 39 or 40, and I must have taken Oklahoma to cover that spread, because when an official on the sideline missed a call that went against the Sooners late in the game, I went ballistic. Replays showed an Oklahoma receiver had caught the ball and moved well up the field for a first down. The linesman blew the call; he thought the player went out of bounds to make the catch. The official's call nullified what would have been a large gain by Oklahoma, setting them up for another score and thus allowing them to cover the spread. His decision ended the Sooner's drive. Oklahoma punted while me and countless others on the wrong side of the bet were shit out of luck.

It's possible it was an over/under bet, and I had taken the over. Over/under is when you predict whether the total number of points scored in a game will be over or under a number set by the bookies. If the Las Vegas line on the over/under was forty-one and only thirty-seven points were scored, the "under" would win. If more than forty-one points were scored, the "over" would win. In this case, it would have been the under that won, and I may have taken the over.

Either way, I remember thinking I needed to find out the name of that football official so I could write him, or the Western Athletic Conference, or whoever, a letter. Or even for a few seconds, threaten him. That's the mindset of a gambler.

There's a reason at least one college or professional football game is on TV every day of the week from late August through December, and there's one reason why those games get viewers every single night of the week. Gambling.

I knew one tragic gambling victim.

I don't have his kids' permission, nor do I want it, nor do I want to share his misfortune by name. Let's call him Ernie. Ernie was a sweetheart, the proverbial man's man, and a great guy to hang out with. Most of our conversations were about women and football. We'd drink beer, laugh our asses off, watch sports.

Ernie hung out with our little group of fans, commentators, and low-level gamblers. We'd get together and create PGA pools for the major golf tournaments. It was during an era when drawing the right number out of a cap and getting the first overall draft pick meant taking Tiger Woods — it also meant you'd already won. Didn't matter, it was an excuse for the fellas to get together four times a spring and summer, throw a little money on the table, and drink beer.

Gradually, unbeknownst to us, Ernie was betting more and losing more. To deal with it, he was drinking more, as in, smelly-breath-at-lunchtime type drinking. This wasn't the Ernie we knew. Ernie lost a lot wagering on his alma mater, a football program that had flared for a decade as a powerhouse, only to fizzle out. He lost to the point of having to get a total of four different mortgages/lines of credit on his home. How did he pull that off? He was a widely respected member of the community, he was a legit business guy, and most of all, he was just Ernie.

It was in that home that Ernie drank himself to death. Bled his liver. A crown and coke in his clutches while sitting at his desk, a gallon-drum of empty half gallons sitting in the garage. While hiding behind sunglasses, I cried like a child at his memorial service, looking at photos of Ernie riding a horse as a kid and floating in the river with his own kids. Fighting the lump in my throat was actually painful; mostly because his death was completely unnecessary. Gambling had beaten him literally into the ground.

Other friends I know didn't take it that far: they went bankrupt — or just short of it — joined a support group, and quit with the help of peers. One buddy I have has been going to a group for almost two decades. Not only has it kept him from placing a wager, it's also brought him another group of close friends to hang out with and . . . not gamble.

I've known a few small-time bookies and one big-time bookie. He just smiled as he backpacked around the big city, collecting thousands from businessmen who blew wads of cash over the weekend. When they win, he also smiles, cordially handing over their winnings into excited hands. He knows he'll be back.

When a "player" wins a $100 bet, he wins $100. When he loses, he loses $110. This is called the "juice." Add 10 percent to all of your losing wagers. That's how it works and how the house money adds up. For the big book-makers who control the betting lines, or the ones below that who modify their lines based on the wagers from their clientele, the idea is to get half the gamblers to bet one way and the other half to bet the opposite. That's why lines change during the week. If it's Kentucky six points over Purdue, and everyone is betting Purdue, then as the days go by leading up to the game, the line might move to Kentucky by four. They're trying to entice more people to bet on Kentucky. In the perfect world, if $100,000 is bet on Kentucky, and $100,000 is bet on Purdue, the bookie knows the bet is a wash for them, or a break even. But they still make the $10,000 in juice from the side that lost.

Naturally, it would be rare to see almost the exact amount bet on each side, but the closer they can get to half and half on a specific wager, the more the juice is worth. Then multiply that times sixty college games and fifteen or sixteen pro games every week, and you get volume.

Some estimate as much as $380 billion changes hands illegally per year on sports in North America, mostly out of the hands of the gamblers.

For an individual bettor, the juice adds up. Five dollars on fifty dollars doesn't sound like a lot, but amateur gamblers tend to always bet a handful of games. It's more fun that way. So if they bet eight games at fifty bucks each and go four and four, they've broken even on the wagers but lost twenty dollars on juice. If they go five wins and three losses, they'd win $100, minus the fifteen dollars juice on the losses, and end up winning eighty-five dollars.

I never think about it. It's water under the bridge, and I can't change the past. If you're someone who is in the middle of a struggle like this, quit now and don't look back. Don't think you'll win it back either. That's the mentality of a man or woman sitting in a casino at a blackjack table who keeps getting free drinks and buying chips. Forget it. Learn the guitar, teach yourself French, spend more time with your kid(s). You'll be glad you did. Don't ruin your family, don't kill yourself, and don't be so freaking selfish. If you're trying to make a quick buck, don't. Work, and make a bunch of slow ones.

And if you stop watching games because of this, you're not really missing out. Watching your favourite sport or team is one thing, to most everyone else involved it's just a business.

———————————

Problem with gambling? Find help 24/7 in the U.S., Canada, and the U.S. Virgin Islands. 1-800-522-4700.

BACK SPASMS

The common medical malady "back spasms" is the most anemic, misleading term in sports medicine history. They should be called "twisting knife in the spine-asms," or "oh my God, it hurts to cough-asms." I had them pretty good the summer of 1997.

As part of my duties with the Boise Hawks baseball club, Idaho's short-season, A-ball farm team for the California Angels, I produced, wrote, and hosted twenty episodes of a weekly thirty-minute TV show called *Hawk Talk*. For episode one in 1996, I decided to go big: skydiving with the coaching staff.

Manager Tom "Kotch" Kotchman would have nothing to do with it; I believe his exact words were "Fuck off" while pitching coach Jim "Benny" Bennett and hitting instructor Todd "Clausy" Claus said yes. We were off to Snake River Skydive with cameraman Dave "Go F' Yourself" Falcone.

Having jumped from a not-so-perfectly-good airplane in Hawaii two years prior, I did my best to reassure the fellas that everything would be just fine. Clausy asked legitimate questions and seemed to show no fear. Benny, the Northwest League's answer to Sam Malone from *Cheers*, started to get very quiet. He wasn't about to back out, but as the airplane motor fired up, his face went completely blank and I honestly thought he might faint.

I went first. The plane wasn't big enough to handle more than one tandem pair at a time. I would be leaping with a guy named Larry strapped to my back. Larry suggested that since I had jumped before, I *should* be able to handle pulling the rip cord on his signal. I agreed.

"Yeah, that sounds good."

Dave attached a wireless microphone to my lapel and taped it down, zipping the jumpsuit up over most of the cord. Based on distance and reception, he'd only be able to hear what I was saying during the final stages of descent, maybe the last couple hundred feet. The idea was for me to do a flying stand-up, an on-camera hit describing part of the show. I think in this case I was supposed to say something like, "When we come back, Jim Bennett and Todd Claus take the plunge." Then we'd land.

I was a wee bit nervous as the plane climbed but, honestly, much of the lustre was gone. They say you never forget the first time. No doubt about it. During the Hawaii jump in March 1994, I was freaked out and speechless during the climb, and I remember practically every little detail. This time, I was slightly blasé, the old "been there, done that." Plus, while this section of Idaho was rather scenic, it wasn't nearly as dramatic from the air as the rest of the state, and not nearly as delightful as the North Shore of Oahu.

We jumped. We dropped at about a hundred miles per hour for thirty-five seconds or so, and then Larry signalled in front of my face for me to pull the chute. Of course, I wasn't paying any attention. I was looking all over the place, turning my head to the right and left and checking out the scenery. To avoid us becoming a human puddle, Larry had no choice but to reach around and rip the cord.

Meanwhile, I, his human air cushion, was in dipshit land. This was exactly why inexperienced skydivers first jump tandem — so someone remembers to pull the chute.

When Larry pulled the cord, I wasn't quite back in the skydive posture. My head was turned sideways and angled up, my arms not completely extended in the neutral position. When the chute opened, our bodies and legs swung down violently and, with a tremendous yank, we went from falling very fast to hardly moving at all.

"Bdddddddddddddd!" Every vertebra in my back cracked. A good crack, the kind you get when someone adjusts it or walks on it. Except near the bottom of my spine; that's where I had a problem. Something strained and I went, "Ughhh!"

I managed to pull off some on-camera audio as we gradually lost altitude. But as I drifted closer to terra firma, Dave not only heard, "When we come back to the show," he also heard, "Aw, shit that hurts," and "Damn, that ain't right!"

Benny jumped, landed, and immediately wanted to jump again. Clausy jumped, landed, and also wanted to do another jump right away. There's nothing like plummeting to the Earth like a rock and then suddenly becoming a glider. The sound of air rushing past one's head is intensely loud until the parachute opens. It's replaced by almost complete silence. That's the most dramatic sensation: loud as hell, quiet as heaven, gliding like a bird.

We interviewed the fellas, did some stand-ups to close the show, and drove off with a pretty darn good local TV show in our hands.

As the summer wore on, the bulging disc in my lower back grew larger. As 1996 rolled into 1997, it began to push on my sciatic nerve. By the 1997 baseball season, I was in trouble.

Ah, sciatica — a dream come true. Pain, constant aggravation, can't sneeze without swerving off the road, can't cough without swearing afterwards, wifey always on top. It made the menial tasks like getting out of bed and walking completely miserable.

Our team medical trainer, Todd Hine, who also worked for the local hockey team during the winter, was tremendously helpful and diligent in trying to relieve my pain and discomfort. He gave me stretching exercises, sent me to a therapist, and attempted to stretch me out himself on a regular basis.

Now, I'm familiar with physical therapy, sports trainers, and the concept of doing whatever is necessary to stretch someone out. But "Hiner" took it to the limit. Since we both travelled with the team, we were together with the rest of the baseball staff practically every day for three months. Each and every day before or during batting practice, Hiner would tell me to lie down on the outfield grass in foul territory, and he'd attempt to stretch my legs and back. The idea was to reduce the pressure on my spine and nerves.

At its simplest, it meant pulling my bent leg by the knee up towards my head to work the hamstring. At its worst, it must have resembled a dry hump.

Once, down the left-field line in Salem, Oregon, manager Kotchman, a hard-core, win-at-all-costs baseball man who, when perturbed, used to call me "Moose Breath," walked by and asked, "What the fuck are you two doing?"

I was on my back, my left leg was somehow up over my chest, and my foot was dangling in the air over my right shoulder. Hiner was lying on top of me.

"Jesus, Hiner, this is ridiculous, careful down there," I'd say, laughing almost uncontrollably while trying to breathe.

"Quiet," he'd say. "You gotta stretch. *Stretch*." Hiner was five-foot-ten; me, a little over six-foot-six.

"Holy shit, get off me," I'd beg. The therapy-molestation would last three or four minutes.

The stretching helped for the short term. I was also sneaking off and visiting a couple of chiropractors on the side. The first guy, Victor, a Canadian-born hockey fan, was actually pretty good. He'd give me adjustments and provide relief. The second guy, some Neanderthal recommended to me by the team owner's son, was not so good.

Long-time, very successful Boise Hawks
manager Tom Kotchman in Salem, Oregon.

I'd lie on my side and he'd slam down on the back of my
rib cage with his chest. This was supposed to "pop" things
back into place. I'm pretty sure my bulging disc was on its
way to herniating.

Come September, the Hawks were where they usually
were at the end of each season: in first place in the four-
team North Division. Their record of fifty-one wins and
twenty-five losses earned them the right to play the winner
of the South Division in a best-of-five Northwest League
championship series. This time around, the Hawks would
meet the Portland Rockies.

It's very rare at the short-season, A-ball level to fly anywhere. Normally, we'd travel overnight by bus. But given
the fact that the Hawks were perennial winners, had once
again earned a spot in the battle for the title, and had taken

a 2–0 series lead on their home field in Boise, owner Bill Pereira bucked up and flew us to Portland. They won Game One 7–5 and Game Two 7–1, so finishing off the Rockies seemed like just a formality. The Hawks would have three chances, if necessary, to pick up the deciding third win on the road. We flew to Portland, Oregon, on September 7. Little did I know that I wouldn't be flying back.

The Hawks disappointed in Game Three, losing 2–1. Two nights later, they failed to lock up the championship again with a 6–0 loss. The series was tied at two and the collars were getting tight. The soon-to-be winningest manager in Northwest League history and his team were on the precipice of an unfathomable collapse.

After Game Four, my broadcast partner, Tommy Smith, and I headed out for a few beers at the Kingston Bar and Grill, a watering hole best described as a sports pub. It stood across the street from Civic Stadium, the Rockies' home ballpark, just steps into the hilly, southwest quadrant of Portland. It had great burgers, chicken sandwiches, and microbrews and was just a couple blocks from our hotel.

After lamenting the possibility of the Hawks not winning a championship, yet revelling in the excitement of having the opportunity to call the deciding game of a championship series the next day, Tommy and I went our separate ways. He went drinking with Hiner and Clausy while I headed back to the hotel to drop off our radio equipment and then meet my brother's brother-in-law, John McDonald.

Johnny was a starving artist, originally from the upper peninsula of Michigan, a "Yooper." By day, he worked in a bookstore as a stock guy, and by night, he'd occasionally play solo acoustic gigs at various venues around crispy, crunchy-granola Portland. Each time the Hawks came for a visit, I'd meet up with him and buy him a few beers at a tiny, triangular, basement bar that sat in the middle of a fork in the road on Burnside Street.

When I set down the box of radio gear in my hotel room, I remember feeling a slight twinge in my back, a twinge above and beyond the normal spasms I'd grown accustomed to. Undaunted, I trotted out to meet Johnny at the bar. We laughed it up, chatted with a few of the locals, and each drank about five or six beers. Besides catching a buzz, I was also going about the business of dehydrating myself with alcohol. My bad back, my drinking, and my not-so-heavy lifting earlier were all about to rendezvous for a memorable rebellion.

Most of the motels we used in the Northwest League were of the Super 8–Ramada Inn–Best Western ilk. Something a middle-class family of four would stay in on a driving trip across the country. Only on rare occasions would our motel be upgraded to a hotel. Portland was one of these times. Not glamorous by any stretch, I think it earned the "hotel" distinction simply because it had more than three storeys. This building had five.

Also rare in this case was the fact that Tommy and I had our own bedrooms. In most places, we shared a motel room with two twin beds and a tiny bathroom. Here, we had a main room off the common balcony entrance, a bathroom to the right, and two separate bedrooms. Tommy's was to the right; I was to the left behind the living area.

When I came home from the bar, I went straight to bed. It was probably midnight, and Tommy hadn't arrived back. I closed the bedroom door and turned in.

Normally, as we all know, one wakes up in a variety of relatively routine ways. One might arise gently and naturally after a good night's rest, or be startled out of a nightmare, or awakened by a barking dog or a loud noise.

Physically, the usual occurrences might include an arm, leg, or hand feeling "dead" or having "fallen asleep" after being slept on funny. For a man, the potential also exists to wake up sporting a Woodrow after enjoying a pleasant dream of some sort. Both of those sensations are much more pleasant than the one that awakened me.

Apparently, I had rolled over or twisted in my sleep just enough to herniate my bulging disc. It essentially blew out, the pieces pressing against my spinal cord and the particles scattering down my spinal column.

I woke up screaming! I was experiencing unbelievable pain and disbelief at the same time. The level of my anguish was alien; I had never come remotely close to suffering this type of acute and protracted agony. It was like a chef was using my lower vertebrae to sharpen a paring knife. I couldn't move.

"Oh my God, this is insane," I said to myself. "Tommy! Tommy! Tommy!" I tried in vain to wake up my passed-out broadcast partner through two closed doors. Mustering enough voice was impossible. The act of yelling caused slight movement; slight movement brought excruciating pain.

It took me the next twenty minutes just to strategize how I was going get to the floor, and another fifteen to reach it. I managed to roll over onto my stomach, inch my way to the edge of the bed, and then "walk" off the end of the bed using my arms and hands as legs and feet. I lowered myself to the floor like finishing a push-up, with my feet scraping down the edge of the bed to the floor.

The good news: I knew I wasn't dying. The bad news: I couldn't stand up, I couldn't crawl on my hands and knees (yet), and there'd be no using the potty.

My endorphins, the body's natural painkillers, had kicked in a little bit, but still not enough to allow me to do anything but belly-crawl. This I did, out into the little hallway, past the bathroom, and into the main room. It took about a half-hour, between gasps, grunts, and groans.

This is when I started to get really concerned about the ball game and the broadcast. It was six a.m., which meant I had about eight hours to get ready for the two p.m. start. Conventional wisdom dictated that I should skip the game, but there was no way I was missing the chance to call the deciding contest for the championship.

I was determined to figure out a way to get on the air. While I should have been worried about someday walking again, or taking a dump, or at least getting off the floor of this Portland hotel room, I was more worried about the show. I was the lead broadcaster in just my second season at a new gig, this was my first championship series of any kind, and my fellow broadcaster, Tommy Smith — fresh out of Santa Clara University and who normally did the play-by-play for innings four, five, and six — simply wasn't very good. That's not stating something Tommy didn't know. He got the job mainly because he had a relative in the ownership group, and it was a one-season experiment heading into the summer. Tommy's uncle Pete, a great guy and a very understanding investor when it came to his nephew's broadcast limitations, was open-minded about the end result: if he were decent, they'd keep him. It didn't help that Tommy was replacing my very accomplished partner from 1996, Jon Sciambi, a guy who went on to call baseball games regularly on ESPN.

I loved Tommy like a little brother, and still do, but there was no way I wanted him soloing for the final game of the Hawks championship series.

I lay on the floor of the hotel room in front of the TV for two hours waiting to call Hiner. I didn't want to wake him up *too* early following a night out, but I needed some ice.

"Dude, my back exploded, you gotta get down here quick," I begged Hiner.

"What? Hold on."

Hiner came and took a look. He had a good chuckle, knowing my life wasn't in danger, ran out, and a few minutes later returned with a bag of ice.

I lay there for another two hours until Tommy finally rolled out of the sack. He burst out laughing.

"Dude, what the hell is going on?" he said.

"Dude, my back blew up," I said.

He felt bad and thought it was funny at the same time.

"Dude, no way."

We said "dude" a lot in 1997.

With that, he asked me if dude needed anything, stepped over me, and headed out to get breakfast. He brought me back some McDonald's. A few minutes later, Hiner brought me a fresh ice pack and some meds.

"Can you crawl yet?" he asked.

I could. And I did. Out the door, along the outdoor balcony that ran in front of all the rooms, into the elevator (where I had a delightful conversation with a fellow hotel guest while staring at his ankle), through the lobby, across the hotel's driveway, and onto the back seat of a Boise Hawks employee's Suburban.

All the while, Tommy and Ryan Brach, the Suburban's owner, walked alongside me, carrying my garment bag and the radio equipment. Only twice did Brach have the nerve to say, "Heel."

Although I could crawl, I couldn't sit — it put too much direct weight on my lower back. I wouldn't be flying home with the team the next day; even if I could sit, I couldn't get up to walk onto the airplane.

Fortunately, because this was the championship series, Brach and a couple other front-office employees had driven the six and a half hours to Portland, and, fortunately for me, they hadn't come in a pick-up truck.

The plan was in place: when the game was over, I'd crawl into the back seat of the Suburban, lie down, and ride 430 miles straight to a hospital in Boise.

Another break in my favour came thanks to old Civic Stadium being a bizarre ballpark. Among its idiosyncrasies, the press box and our broadcast position were at field level behind home plate. Fellow broadcasters referred to it as Eva Braun's bunker (as in Hitler's wife): cement floor, blue cement walls, and a wire cage to look through about twenty feet behind home plate. Calling balls and strikes was great, depth perception, not so much. A broadcaster would have to wait to describe balls hit in the air to avoid calling an infield pop-up a fly ball to right, or a home run a line drive to left. It was simply difficult to pick up distance off the bat.

The great thing about the location on this occasion: I didn't have to crawl up sixty steps to a traditional press box. A driveway ran right down into the guts of the building behind the bunker. I crawled out of the Suburban, into the press box, and lay across two chairs. For the game itself, I lay on the counter where we'd normally keep our notes and broadcast equipment. I called innings one, two, three, seven, eight, and nine lying sideways with my right arm propping up my headset-laden cranium.

Lounging like a Kardashian, all six-and-a-half feet of me was stretched out, face pressed up against the screen — a minor-league diva. The counter was only about twenty inches wide. At one point, manager Kotchman, who walked by after talking to the ump or something, stopped and stared at me like I had six eyeballs.

He must have thought, *What the hell is wrong with this guy?*

"I screwed up my back," I tried to explain through the screen.

"Uh, huh." This confirmed his suspicions about my overall mental stability.

The ball game didn't go so well. For me, the next three hours were literally the dictionary definition of adding insult to injury. At one point, with a chance to tie the game in the top of the sixth, Boise base runner Paxton Stewart got doubled off second base when he took off running on a pop-up to left field. That was after his walk and a base hit to start the inning. Ugly. The Hawks lost Game Five 4–2, and the series.

No championship, no ring, no nothing — but the disappointment would have to wait. I was actually relieved to be crawling into the Suburban to start the long ride home.

Cell phones were rare in 1997, but we had one on this occasion, which was nice when the fellas decided to stop in Pendleton, Oregon, halfway along our journey, to gamble at the Wild Horse Casino. They ran in for about forty-five minutes while I lay on a bag of ice in the back seat chatting on the phone with my wife, Nora, who planned on meeting me at the hospital.

Talk about taking one for the team: acutely injured guy lying alone in the back of a truck while his buddies played blackjack. Actually, I thought it was kind of funny, and it was the least I could do, given how much I appreciated the lift, and because the boys cancelled overnight plans in Portland to drag my gimpy ass home.

Three hours after the gambling stop, we pulled up to St. Alphonsus Regional Medical Center in Boise. My wife walked up and thanked my colleagues, while an orderly with a gurney came outside to get me. I crawled from seat to stretcher.

Once inside, the nurse on duty wasn't buying into the seriousness of my back problem. To find out just how bad it was, she gave me a shot of something, Demerol I think, into my right butt cheek.

"In a few minutes, I'll have you get up and we'll check it out," she said.

Oh really? Take your time. After what seemed like just a few moments, I was flyin'.

"Yeah, baby," I said to Nora. "Oh yeah, this stuff is gooooood." I was on Pluto. The pain was absolutely gone — until the nurse had me stand up.

"Ouch, ah, damn! Oh, no, no, no. Can't do it," I said.

"Really?" she answered. "Well, let me give you one more shot on the other side, and we'll check again."

"Works for me." I smiled as I lay back down. Moments later, my happy-happy, joy-joy buzz was revitalized. This was an acute, high-potency shot of painkiller pretty close to the nerve centre.

"Oh yeah, I gotta get me some of this," I said, laughing, to Nora.

"Knock it off," she ordered, smiling.

"Man, I'm tellin' ya!"

The nurse came back in.

"Okay. Get up."

Nope. Again, once I stood up and tried to move around upright, the pain crashed the party in my extra-terrestrial brain.

"Alright," the nurse determined, "you're going for an MRI right now."

Upon further review, the doctor determined that surgery was required almost immediately. I was admitted to the hospital as a patient, my first time since birth. The next morning, I'd have a partial discectomy.

Lying on the operating table, looking up into a light, I saw the face of the anaesthesiologist as she put a mask over my nose and mouth.

"Okay," she said. "Count down from ten."

"Ten, nine, eight, seven . . ."

Tommy Smith married his college sweetheart, Shannon, is in the medical sales business in Arizona, and has four kids.

Kotch is managing in the Gulf Coast League in the Boston Red Sox organization.

Clausy is the global scouting coordinator for the Red Sox.

At last word, Benny was coaching baseball in Australia.

Hiner owns a training center outside of Boise.

> "I'm not never gonna be crushed by anything that happens . . . because I take life day by day."

Earvin "Magic" Johnson, March 1981
(a decade prior to his HIV announcement)

THE PEEWEE PRESS

I had a few zits and my voice hadn't completely changed. My buddy Ric's voice *really* hadn't changed. We'd tease him with Mickey Mouse comparisons.

He was sixteen, in the visitors locker room after a Detroit Pistons game, when he approached New York Knicks forward Toby Knight.

"Toby, can I ask you a few questions?"

"Nnnnnnnnnnnnnnnnnnnnnnnnnnnnnnnnnnno," Knight answered and smiled.

"Really?" Ric followed.

"No, go ahead."

"What was the difference tonight that allowed the Knicks to win tonight?" Ric asked.

"Well, on the scoreboard, we had more total points than they did, thus it was a victory for New York," Knight answered. "Ha, ha."

"Really?" Ric held his ground. "You guys have been coming around lately, playing better ball."

Toby finished chuckling and then straightened up.

"We were struggling for a while, playing hot and cold, and the team is starting to get a bit . . . come together, and we've got it coming along. Tonight was a good . . . an indication of better ball," Knight concluded.

"Thanks," Ric said.

Every once in a while, a player would mess with us like that or ask a question in response to our first question.

"How old are you?" they'd say.

We'd explain how we worked for a high-school radio station and also for a professional station, under the table, getting post-game sound.

"Well, that's cool," they'd respond.

The defining moment of our first season occurred when that grumpy old rent-a-cop who guarded the press room entrance saw Ric and me approaching before a game and announced for all the world to hear, "Here comes the peewee press." He had what we call "summer teeth" in hockey: "summer here and summer there." He grinned from ear to ear; neither Ric nor I was laughing.

The idea over the course of time was to gradually shake the "peewee" off the press. This would involve being patient while keeping our ears open and our mouths shut.

Early in our journalistic career, at the end of the

1979–80 season, we were witness to an event common to anyone covering pro basketball, or any sport for that matter: watching someone get fired. Detroit coach Richie Adubato was the first person I ever observed getting ousted. He had replaced Dick Vitale twelve games into the campaign, moving up from an assistant coach position. When Adubato took over the Pistons, he inherited a team in shambles.

The Pistons had traded M.L. Carr and a first-round draft pick to Boston for Bob McAdoo. McAdoo quickly earned the nickname "Mc-A-Don't." The former scoring champ and superstar spent a portion of his first two seasons in Detroit sitting on the bench with a sore foot and an injured groin.

Detroit also dumped longtime fan favourite, Bob Lanier. They sent him to Milwaukee for Kent Benson. Eric Money came from Philadelphia, little-used Steve Malovic from Washington, and "Kamikaze" Ron Lee came from Atlanta. Among the injured players: James McElroy, Greg Kelser, and Terry Duerod. Duerod, Terry Tyler, and John Long had all followed Coach Vitale from the University of Detroit. Tyler and Long lasted a bit; Duerod didn't.

With all this instability, it's not surprising that under Adubato, the Pistons would win just twelve ball games. They finished the season with sixteen wins and sixty-six losses, and when it was over, Adubato was finished.

When the final home game of the season ended, I was sullen. I knew it would be five months before I had the surreal opportunity again to interview people like Julius Erving, Larry Bird, and Magic Johnson.

However, after spending time in the locker room that

evening, I completely forgot about my own petty concerns. Instead, I stood by and watched a ritual that takes place every year, in every league, in a handful of cities: a head coach being let go. Adubato was brought in as an "interim" coach, and he wasn't about to hold the job, with only two road games left in a disastrous season. His impending departure gave me a strange feeling. What if something like this happened to my dad?

A farewell banner, which had hung from the middle level of the Silverdome, signed by dozens of fans, had been brought down and draped inside the little room where Adubato conducted his interviews. A few Pistons employees stuck their heads in to wish the coach well. As the postgame interviews wrapped up, I hung out to listen to the last few questions and comments. Richie was a man let go, a two-game lame duck, a man without a team, a man forced to say farewell. I was a little bit sad and a lot more contemplative. I wondered what Adubato would do next.

Less than a year later, I saw him holding a post-game beer in the visitors locker room at the Silverdome as an assistant coach with the Atlanta Hawks.

That same season, year two of our little pro-sports endeavour, Ric and I began to get much more comfortable. Of course, as teenagers, we still had to mind our "p's and q's." For example, I had no right to argue with an NBA head coach. I had no right to doubt him, question him, or even talk to him for that matter. I knew very little about life in the NBA, let alone about how to coach a professional basketball team. But there I stood, in fantasy land, playing reporter.

Pistons coach Scotty Robertson knew I was young,

naïve, and maybe too ignorant to make a difference. When I stepped over the imaginary line, he quickly let me know it.

Led by rookies Isiah Thomas and Kelly Tripucka, the Pistons had just beaten the Chicago Bulls on the day after Christmas, 1981.

"How do you look at the games coming up on the road?" I asked. "Teams you can beat?"

Robertson, Chuck Daly's predecessor as head coach of the Pistons, responded, "Welllll . . . teams what?"

"Teams you can beat, I mean pretty eas . . . " My voice trailed under his.

"I . . . I . . . I don't know where the hell you . . . you're . . . you're new. You know. Teams we can beat pretty easily? There ain't nobody in this league like that. I'm not trying to put you down now, but you're wrong. If you . . . if you check the record lately you'd find that New Jersey and Washington are on a pretty darn good roll. And there ain't no teams in this league that you can beat easily, much less *we* can beat easily. They're gonna be tough ball games, they're on the road, and we're gonna have to play well."

Ouch.

Scotty then mellowed a bit and went on for another twenty seconds about how his team was playing well and that a couple other teams in the division had injury problems. I wasn't listening. I was still hurting as I firmly held the microphone in front of his mouth. Charlie Vincent of the *Detroit Free Press* had a patient look on his face, combined with a smirk. George Eichorn of WXYZ Radio was standing next to me. Two veterans watching me get lambasted.

Ouch, ouch, ouch. *Was it something I said, or just how I said it? That wasn't a stupid question, was it? What a jerk — the Pistons had won four in a row. I'm not new, I've been here covering these games for two years.* All of these thoughts raced through my mind as I carried my injured pride out of the locker room and into the tunnel.

Just when I might have been getting comfortable, or even complacent, getting a little cocky about being a kid covering the Pistons, I got knocked back on my ass.

Other times, the heated exchanges with the coach were fun, like two weeks later, following a loss to Boston.

"Why'd you take John Long out so early in the third quarter?"

"Because he asked to come out. He was tired."

"I take it you thought the officiating was pretty poor tonight?"

"No, I thought it was terrific," Robertson snarled. Tense laughter followed. Coaches don't like to be asked about the refs. They usually say they can't blame a crappy game on the officials. Plus, bad-mouthing the officials in the media isn't good policy or popular with the League.

Of the three years Ric and I covered the Pistons regularly, year three, the 1981–82 season, was by far the most exciting. Thomas was the second overall pick in the first round of the draft, after Mark Aguirre to Dallas. Tripucka came later in the first round, out of Notre Dame. The Pistons were making a serious rebuilding effort and fans in the Motor City were pumped.

Two images of Isiah Thomas stick in my mind from his first season.

First: his shy, humble, baby-faced demeanour with

the press. Throughout his career he was generally known for being soft spoken and for flashing his pearly whites as he talked. We'd find out later in his career that this was just one half of "Zeke." He actually wielded a great deal of power in the organization as the team's best player. He was tough, focused, and determined.

I knew him back then as a sweet-moving, sweet-talking, (sometimes) crybaby rookie. His humility coming out of Indiana as a sophomore was impressive, but tough to swallow, given his importance to the team.

Let's face it, Isiah was the main reason the Pistons went from twenty-one wins in 1980–81 to thirty-nine wins in 1981–82.

"I think this team would survive without me, they'd go on living," explained Thomas following a six-point win against New Jersey in November 1981. The Pistons were three-and-oh.

"Living, but winning?" pursued writer Vincent.

"Yes, I think so," replied Thomas.

"So what in your mind would be the difference between last year, and this start?"

"I don't know," Thomas answered, "I didn't see this team last year, and I have no idea how good a club they were last year."

"Not very," Vincent volleyed.

"Sorry . . . ha, hee hee." Thomas smiled.

"You're reluctant to take the credit?"

"Yes, I am, because it's not because of me . . . it's because of everyone. It's a team effort. Um, other guys play well too, it's not because I'm playing well that we're winning, it's because everyone's playing well that we're winning."

Comments like that made Thomas a very popular young player in blue-collar Detroit.

The second image of Thomas that lingers in my mind in his rookie year: the time he injured his knee. They carried him out of the locker room and stuffed him into the back seat of his Mercedes, which had been pulled down into the tunnel. Zeke was gimpy, and the grimace on his face told the story. The car seemed to soothe him. This young dude was earning some serious cash.

If only young radio reporters were getting paid the same as young basketball players. I took solace in the fact that although our paycheques had nothing in common, we were both having a really good time.

Larry Bird was the first player who made me realize just how monotonous it was for these ball players to answer pretty much the same questions night in and night out, especially for star players, like Bird, who automatically were approached by at least a half-dozen media types after every game. He answered quickly, succinctly, and in a monotone voice, like a computer with a rural Indiana twang. To me, that made it more imperative to ask him smart questions.

All in all, considering I was a tall, goofy, teenage reporter full of inexperience, most of the players were very gracious in answering my questions. The first to really put me at ease was Rick Barry, a superstar finishing up his career with the Houston Rockets.

I was covering my second game ever on January 19, 1980. A couple of nights before, Barry had eclipsed the 25,000-point mark in career scoring.

"Can I ask you a few questions?" I started.

"Sure, go ahead," Barry replied.

"First of all, congratulations on your 25,000 Wednesday night. Also, first of all, I'd like to say, on your three-pointers, have you been practicing that a lot in practice, because you hit a couple tonight?"

"Yeah, I've been practicing a little bit more since the coach has been using it a little bit more, as far as the offense is concerned. I don't go out there and spend all day shooting them, I feel I can shoot from that range — it's a shot you have to pick a good time to use. It can be helpful if used at the right time, if the ball goes in the basket. If you go out there and start firing them up indiscriminately, you can get your ball club in trouble. It's the type of shot that if it goes in . . . if it doesn't and you don't get the rebound, it's trouble. It's tough to put an evaluation on it."

What a solid answer from a true pro, to a nervous question from a dorky kid with chronic Peter Tork (of The Monkees) hair.

Interestingly, Barry's career numbers benefitted just briefly from the three-point shot. His NBA predecessors didn't have it, while those who followed him would. The rule change, implemented for the 1979–80 season, created a statistical subtlety in the record books that would forever affect comparisons between the eras.

Barry went on to discuss the rumours of his impending retirement and the fact that he would continue his career as a TV analyst and possibly as an actor once he finished up as a ball player. He retired after that season.

It was the first time I forgot whom I was talking to and where I was, and completely concentrated on the questions and the answers. Gradually, I came to realize that professional athletes were just like anyone else and that there was no reason to be intimidated. I was still learning, but I was confident in my abilities. If someone was a jerk, that was okay. A basketball player can be grumpy after a tough day on the job, just like an auto worker or an accountant.

Kareem Abdul-Jabbar *always* seemed a bit grumpy. Not so much from a rough-and-tumble night on the court, but from the "veteran-tired-of-reporters" syndrome. A superstar, a six-time NBA Most Valuable Player, Abdul-Jabbar spent season after season as the centre of attention. Having Magic Johnson around helped relieve a bit of the pressure from the press, especially when the Lakers were in Detroit.

On the one occasion I interviewed Abdul-Jabbar, in February 1981, Magic had indeed drawn most of the media. Only one other time had Johnson, the former Michigan State Spartan star, performed professionally in a regular-season game at Detroit, so most reporters flocked to the youngster from Lansing. That opened the door to Abdul-Jabbar for me and WWJ-radio reporter, John Bell. Bell was a nice, soft spoken guy, with a fantastic announcing voice. His mellifluous tones eventually led him to the job as public address announcer at Tiger Stadium.

Bell reached Abdul-Jabbar just ahead of me. The big fellah was sitting on a stool in front of his locker, putting on his socks. Both Bell and I decided to kneel down on one knee in front of him and extend our microphones. Like batters poised in the on-deck circle, we leaned forward and began the questioning. Again, Abdul-Jabbar was not all that excited.

"Sure, go ahead," Jabbar responded to our request to interview him. Then, just as Bell asked his first actual basketball question, Abdul-Jabbar ignored us, and stood up.

"After you've already been the champs . . ." Bell stopped. I was suddenly staring at Abdul-Jabbar's right kneecap; Bell, staring at his left. We both did the slow head tilt upward as Kareem turned to grab more clothing. It was incredible how tall he stood. Our vantage point made it even more ridiculous. Bell and I briefly looked at each other and chuckled. As we made the effort to stand simultaneously, our old friend George Eichorn, then the host of his own show on WBRB radio in nearby Macomb County, Michigan, slid in for a question.

"What did you think of that Piston effort out there tonight? Is it what you expected from the scouting reports you got?" Eichorn asked.

"Gee, you know, they tried hard to win, they played hard," Abdul-Jabbar responded.

"How about down the stretch, you against Wayne Robinson, wasn't that giving away a little too much, huh, from their standpoint?" Eichorn followed with a snicker.

"Well, you know, I don't . . . I don't really get into the coaching part of it. That's what the coach went with, that's his decision."

Bye, George. Abdul-Jabbar didn't appear to enjoy the hometown reporter taking pokes at the Pistons while asking questions. He seemed annoyed by the lack of respect. That meant trouble for Bell when he tried to finish his interrupted question.

"Kareem, you guys had to know coming in here

that . . ." Bell started and was interrupted again. Pistons General Manager Jack McCloskey stepped up to greet Abdul-Jabbar and quickly shake his hand.

"Hey, Jack, how you doin'?" Abdul-Jabbar reacted.

Bell continued again.

"The Pistons are lying there, waitin' for you, it's that way everywhere you go when you become NBA champs . . ."

"Uh huh."

"They knocked off the Sixers, and I know you guys knew that, but still in all, the Pistons are the worst team in the NBA, how do you . . ."

"Well, they have the worst record," Abdul-Jabbar interjected. "But that doesn't necessarily mean what it says."

"How do you guys approach this game? Did you approach it as a tough game, or more like a practice, a warm-up for the big game coming up for you guys?"

Ouch. Bell was getting dangerously close to that dreaded situation where the questions become longer than the answers. Generally, when that happens, things aren't going very well. Abdul-Jabbar dismissed the negativism.

"I . . . I really don't understand what you mean."

I was hurting for, and with, Bell. I also grew impatient. This was my first, and probably last, opportunity to ask Kareem Abdul-Jabbar a question. The big man went on about his dressing business as Bell continued.

"Okay. As the NBA champions, everywhere you go, the Pistons, the Sixers, everyone is trying to knock you off."

"Right."

"When you come in against a team that has only thirteen victories, like Detroit, it's tough to get psyched up, it's tough anyway to get psyched up every night in the NBA, night after night, but against the Pistons especially, isn't it?" Bell concluded.

"Not necessarily, you know, they played us tough out in L.A. We were in quite a fight all the way through the game and, ah, they played hard tonight. They might not have a good record, but that doesn't mean they don't come and do their job," Kareem answered.

"Then that puts pressure on you to do your job every night regardless," Bell followed.

"Well, you know, that's . . . that's what they pay me for. My job doesn't change all that much."

My turn.

"What about the race right now with Phoenix? How does it shape up? What will it take to overtake the Suns?" I asked.

"Well, we gotta continue to play well and we gotta get lucky too. But, that's something that you have to wait and see."

Bell thanked Abdul-Jabbar and bailed. I asked one more question, about Pistons centre Paul Mokeski, and how Abdul-Jabbar rated him. As he responded, I drifted back to thinking about this man's immense height. I stood about six-foot-two at the time. Abdul-Jabbar topped seven feet; a ten- or eleven-inch difference that seemed like a hell of a lot more.

As he finished a kindly comment about Mokeski, I savoured the fact that I was chatting with maybe the greatest player ever. I thanked him, and I wandered off.

Just before I walked out of the Lakers locker room that

With friends Tracy Roberts and Ric Blackwell
at our high school graduation in 1982.

night, I experienced another brief encounter with hoops royalty. The bus engine revved, and the players filed out. As Magic Johnson walked by, chatting with anyone and everyone as he went, I reached out and touched his knee-length fur coat.

"Take it easy, Magic," I said as I patted his back. He didn't respond nor did he even notice as my hand sank into four inches of sable. It was the softest and smoothest thing I had ever felt. My right hand simply disappeared for a moment.

"Holy crap," I almost said aloud. I didn't want to take my fingers off the coat. I wanted to pet the damn thing. Instead, with mouth agape, I just stared at it as Magic walked away.

Ric Blackwell went on to anchor TV sports and news for a number of years on both coasts of Florida and helped me get at least two jobs along the way. He's married with four kids and runs his own production business. He was my best man the first time I got married.

BIG Z ON THE MOUNTAIN Part 1

In the summer of 2008, Boston Bruins Captain, Zdeno Chára, decided to add his name to the list of NHL hockey players involved with the international humanitarian organization Right To Play. Chára, the tallest player in league history, would do this in a fittingly large manner. Not only would he visit underprivileged African children for a few days in Mozambique as an RTP Athlete Ambassador with Calgary Flames defenceman Robyn Regehr, Chára would then stick around and raise awareness for the cause by trekking up Africa's highest mountain, Kilimanjaro, in Tanzania.

The climb involved four other people.

Mark Brender, deputy director of RTP Canada, organized the entire trip and accompanied the hockey players around Mozambique before joining in on the trek. Brender, in a previous life, had traipsed around a portion of the Himalayas.

Darryl Lepik was a producer for NHL Productions/ Studios who leapt at the chance to climb Kilimanjaro. A self-described workout freak, triathlon type, Lepik essentially built the business opportunity to shoot a documentary around the personal opportunity of climbing the mountain. He made the travel and budget arrangements for himself and his camera guy, organized the shoots, and essentially directed the production.

Mark Berg was Lepik's handpicked choice as cameraman. Aside from being affable and talented, Berg was considered in decent-enough shape to handle the climb, and, more importantly, interested in taking on the challenge. He was also paid handsomely.

I was the last adventurer. I had been to Africa to shoot a documentary with Brender and Right To Play the previous summer and was anxious to get involved again. Like Lepik, for whatever reason, I had a profound interest in summiting this mountain. I planned to take part in just the Tanzanian portion of the excursion, promote the cause, and write about it for a handful of media outlets in Boston. For this, I was not paid handsomely. I actually used frequent-flyer mileage to fly round trip to Africa.

At the last minute, I also decided to make this excursion the sixth and final thirty-minute episode of *Hockey*

Mark Berg, Mark Brender, Darryl Lepik, Zdeno Chára.

Odyssey, a pilot TV series, plagued by a limited budget, that aired on the NHL Network.

Berg would be shooting his documentary on high-definition equipment worth tens of thousands of dollars. I'd be shooting on a Panasonic palm-sized camcorder worth about 600 bucks.

It all seemed like a great idea: raise some money and publicity for a good cause and throw in some personal adventure and accomplishment for good measure. Well, as Scottish poet Robert Burns best put it, "The best laid schemes o' mice an' men/Gang aft agley" (often go awry).

The first problem for the fellas: logistics and bureaucracy in the developing world. Despite the fact that they had properly filled out the necessary paperwork in advance, the customs agent they were dealing with upon arrival in Mozambique wasn't going to cooperate. Unsure whether to pay him a bribe and afraid of being arrested if they did, the crew decided to hold their wallets. And without his palm being greased, the customs guy decided not to allow the professional equipment into Mozambique at all. Berg and Lepik were forced to shoot some limited video on their own personal camcorder and to take some still photographs while the HD equipment remained under government sequester. They did get all the gear back as they left the country, but for the first segments of the final product, they had to use their still shots, plus video from the documentary we'd made the previous summer, involving other kids and different hockey players.

Meanwhile, as the first portion of their journey was winding down, I was flying into Nairobi, Kenya, to meet them at the airport. Unfortunately, I arrived fourteen hours ahead of them, and, no, there's not a hell of a lot to do at the Nairobi airport.

Typically in this scenario anywhere else in the world, I'd hop a cab or train to the nearby metropolis. In this case, it wasn't such a good idea. Knowing I was going to be in Kenya for just that day and a brief layover on the way home, I didn't really want to change any money. More importantly, the crime rate in Nairobi was off the charts at this time, and a popular pastime was the kidnapping of foreign tourists.

Thus, I slept on and off in a chair in the "business class" lounge, drank tea intermittently, ate crackers, and occasionally took a lap around the portion of the airport in which I was allowed. Fortunately, Wimbledon was in full swing and I watched a lot of tennis on an international sports channel, and some bizarre foreign movies when the channel was changed.

When I met with my four compadres before boarding our evening connection to Kilimanjaro, the crew was speechless with frustration. Lepik and Berg explained the aforementioned TV camera trauma. Berg was particularly stressed out, still concerned that his equipment had almost been permanently seized.

The conversation then turned to Diamox (acetazolamide), the anti-altitude-sickness medication. I explained how I had taken, at the advice of my doctor, four pills in the morning and four in the afternoon each of the last two days in preparation for the climb, and how the stuff made me have to piss like I had something angry in my bladder that had to get out.

Brender, in turn, described how his doctor had told him to take eight in the morning and eight more throughout the day, and that it also made him have to pee like a well-hung racehorse.

Berg then said his doctor had told him to take two in the morning, two in the afternoon and two at night, but that he hadn't taken any yet. I suggested he abstain completely to avoid excruciatingly intense, short-notice urination urges. Little did we know at this point just how much our Diamox-taking strategy would impact the success or failure of the overall endeavour. I decided to start taking one pill each morning and one before bed each night, Berg and Brender chose to take them rarely and randomly, while Chára and Lepik opted to forego the preventative medication altogether. We each took it upon ourselves to decide on the appropriate drug regime, given the inconsistencies in our various prescriptions and the fact that we didn't really believe the drug would make a big difference to how we felt on the climb.

Symptoms of altitude sickness can include headache, nausea and dizziness, loss of appetite, fatigue, shortness of breath, general indifference, and disturbed sleep patterns. All of us would eventually experience at least one of these ill effects. The most important key to avoiding these problems, aside from premedication, was gradual acclimatization.

We were less than twenty-four hours from beginning our climb, but we still had to jump on a prop plane from Nairobi to Kilimanjaro Airport in Tanzania. What seemed like a routine connecting journey became anything but for me.

Upon arrival, just beyond the southern slopes of Kili, I discovered my luggage had been lost. Normally, lost luggage involves a relatively minor inconvenience and eventual door-to-door delivery by the offending airline. In sub-Saharan Africa, not so much. My shit was *gone*.

A pair of jeans, some flip flops, maybe a couple shirts, some toiletries — on a trip to Aruba, that would have been okay. But in this case, they had lost my big trek backpack and everything in it. The carefully compiled list of items from Worldwide Quest Agency's pretrip checklist was gone. Hiking boots, heavy boots, winter coat for 19,000 feet, gloves, winter pants, socks, fleece, long-sleeved layers, boxers, sleeping mat, sleeping bag, retractable hiking pole, small first-aid kit, and my toque were all gonzo.

As we rode in the shuttle from the airport to the Marangu Hotel, I took stock.

Okay, we're heading up the mountain tomorrow. I have nothing, and we have no choice but to start. Delaying the trip is not an option. Zdeno Chára (whom I didn't know well at the time, other than his public, hard-ass, hockey-machine persona) *is going to kick my ass if I whine or somehow manage to screw up his trip. Or they're going to climb and I'm gonna go home, or I'll be sitting in Marangu for a week. Horrible.*

I did have my little NBC Torino Olympic carry-on backpack with me. As we pulled up to the lodge, the other guys hopped out with all their tough-guy hiking shit, like Doctor David Livingstone. I hopped out like Dora the Explorer.

"C'mon guys, let's go!" Not so much.

Brender empathized. He was like, "Dude, we'll figure something out."

Chára looked at me like, "You're not screwing up my trip."

Berg looked at me like, "You're not screwing up my trip."

Lepik didn't even bother looking at me.

Bottom line, I had held on to the items I would need to get my job done. I had my notebook and journal. I had writing implements. I had my little still camera, and I had my camcorder with enough backup batteries on hand to document the journey.

In any situation on the road, I always try to make sure the items I'll need to do the job, to perform, are on, or with, my body. I also had my running shoes; a rolled up t-shirt; my lucky, plastic travel lizard my son had given me years before; the clothes I was wearing; and one extra pair of mini-socks that came in the business-class airline kit.

The five of us filed into a large wooden lodge that served as the dining room at the Marangu Hotel, where a couple of local women promptly served us bread, stew, and tea. We were the only ones in the room.

The warm meal and the chance to sit and relax and chat as a group renewed the soul. We would soon be part of the same team, and although we didn't really know what adventure or specific topography lay before us, we sensed we'd forever be bound by this once-in-a-lifetime experience.

The walls were adorned with photographs and art-work of Kilimanjaro and its summit. The most startling realization was just how much the snow lines and glaciers on top of the mountain had receded in recent photos, compared to images from the 1970s and '80s.

The other realization: "Shit, we're going up there?"

Brender and I retired to our nearby cottage, Berg and Lepik to theirs, and Chára to his. As we shut it down for the night, my roommate, Brender, remained confident we'd find a solution for my missing gear.

"Maybe you can buy something," he suggested.

As a delightful African day dawned, it turned out that Brender was mostly right. Instead of buying equipment, I'd be able to rent gear at the base of the mountain at the gate of Marangu National Park. This according to the man we would come to rely on for everything for the next six days, our head guide, a Tanzanian mountain man named Aloyce Manyanga.

I didn't have much in the way of leverage or bargaining power. There was a vendor operating out of a wooden shed in the parking lot just inside the park, offering up all kinds of supplies. I would end up renting most of what I needed for the equivalent of US$240. That seemed like a lot for renting clothes, but with no luggage whatsoever, and my journey beginning in an hour, the African vendor dude kind of had me over a barrel.

I quickly got the feeling I wasn't the first, nor would I be the last, who had lost his luggage on his way to the mountain. Aloyce tried to ease us through the negotiations in Ki-Swahili, and Brender chipped in a portion of the cost because I didn't have the full amount in Tanzanian dollars.

There were still key items missing from my newly acquired kit: a sleeping mat, layers of clothes, extra socks, and hiking boots that fit. The rentals were one size too small. My new teammates would offer up extra bits and pieces as the journey unfolded. Brender lent me an orange long-sleeved, sweat-free shirt, which I wore the entire time. Lepik eventually lent me socks, a winter cap, and gloves; Chára some sweatpants and some first-aid items.

Aloyce had reached the summit of Kili' more than a hundred times. He was a legitimate professional. Unlike some of the shady trek operators who often prey on European teenagers and rush them up the mountain, Aloyce preached patience and determination. We would be taking the second-longest and potentially most scenic route to the top. The less credible guides would hustle groups up what was called the "Coca-Cola" route, a commercial reference to Western tourists. These three-day jaunts directly up the Kibo trail on the southeast side of the mountain from Marangu often led to stories of altitude sickness and failure.

While I was getting familiar with my new supplies, cameraman Berg and producer Lepik were getting familiar with the national park bureaucrats. For a little while, it appeared Berg and his equipment might be headed home. As opposed to seeing it seized for a second time on his trip, he was prepared to just pack it up and go home. After a great deal of angst, a little bit of palm-greasing and pleading, and some intervention from Aloyce, it was determined that, yes, Berg would be able to bring his camera onto the mountain.

With that hurdle cleared, we left what we hoped would be our eventual finish line coming off the mountain, Marangu National Park. We stuffed our equipment, our now six-man group, and a driver into a white Suburban for a miserable four-hour ride to our starting point near the Kenyan border. We wound towards our destination northeast of the mountain on narrow gravel and dirt roads, which eventually became a future highway under construction. The road construction was in its infancy and, based on the lack of progress and the primitive means of development, it was clear that the infancy was going to last a long, long time.

We occasionally passed enormous boulders, idle backhoes, road wideners, or stray animals, but for the most part we passed stray people. No one can afford cars, few can afford bikes, so most Tanzanians walk miles and miles along the side of the road from village to village.

Every person — whether a school kid, an old man, a

family, or a scantily clad professional girl standing very close to the road — every single person would stop what they were doing and watch our van go by and ogle at the foreign occupants. I swear I made eye contact with practically every person we passed. Based partially on my previous experience in Africa, I knew many of these people were desperate for any form of prosperity or escape. It seemed they were trapped in the moving landscape, some dying for an opportunity to jump in the van and ride away.

Being just a few hundred miles from the equator, it was too hot not to ride with the windows cracked open, but with the windows cracked open, the dirt and dust from the roadway poured in. The dry landscape became palpable inside the van. Aloyce's driver was moving along at a pretty good clip, when he didn't have to stop at a narrow section to let an oncoming truck pass or slow down to buck through some enormous ruts in the road. Dust gradually filled our eye sockets, our mouths, our noses, and coated our skin and hair. Once or twice, the driver made a wrong turn and had to be corrected by Aloyce and double back. These unplanned detours were almost unbearable.

Finally, we reached a little wood-and-mud hut village called Nale Moru, in a region called Rongai, near the northeast corner of Tanzania. We turned left off the main road and followed a narrow lane up toward the mountain. About a mile along, we came to a shed, an outhouse, and a camping area where a few dozen African men had congregated. They were mountain porters looking for a gig. From this group, Aloyce would select the twenty or so men who would carry our supplies, food, camping materials, and TV equipment up and down the mountain.

For the six-day trek, most of them would each make a total of about twenty-five bucks. We stood around for a few minutes, took a couple of photographs, and then, suddenly, we were beginning our hike up the lower reaches of Kilimanjaro.

The mountain is actually made up of three peaks. Kibo, or Uhuru, is the highest: the snow-clad dome, the one in all the photos, and the one we were attempting to summit. Local tribes call it the House of God; others call it the roof of Africa. At 19,340 feet, Uhuru Peak is the continent's highest point.

The second peak, Mawenzi, is the next-highest spot, about 3,000 feet shorter than Kibo, and made up of rocky spires. About 800,000 years ago, a decent portion of its northern wall blew away in an eruption, leaving jagged remains behind. East of the main mountain and connected to it by a formation called "the saddle," the crater of Mawenzi would be our last stop before stalking Kibo.

Shira, the third and lowest peak, an extinct volcano, sits in the distance to the west, and wouldn't be a factor in our climb.

With its elevation and the fact that it is a total of fifty miles long and about twenty-six miles wide, Kilimanjaro is the largest free-standing mountain in the world.

Our trail on the first day wasn't unlike the road we had travelled on: pure dust. Not long into the hike, my almost-new Asics running shoes had turned brown. The pace was slow on purpose. Aloyce introduced us to a phrase that he would repeat over and over again during the trip, especially when times got tough, "*pole, pole*" (pronounced "pole-lay, pole-lay"), Swahili for "slow determination."

"No hurry. No hurry in Africa," Aloyce would say.

We climbed gently and consistently through maize and potato fields, and then through dry forest. We hiked for about three and a half hours, ascending 4,000 feet, and then camped in an area of thick underbrush and vegetation just below the encroaching moorland. Our campsite sat at 8,600 feet.

"Hey, Brender," I said, "if this was Idaho, I'd be snowboarding right now. Here, I'm walkin' around in a long-sleeve shirt!"

The porters, who had rushed ahead, had set up our tents, boiled water, and prepared dinner. We ate together in a dinner tent, washed up as best we could, and jumped into our tents at dusk, about 7:00 p.m.

"It was steeper than I thought it was going to be," Chára stated. "Harder than I thought."

During this first day, our cameraman Berg came to a realization: The African mountain porters were permanently acclimated. He wasn't. Thoughts of carrying his own camera up the mountain, mostly out of concern for its well-being, were abruptly discounted as he began getting winded an hour or so into the day's journey. He quickly came to trust the three extra porters hired specifically to tote the TV gear.

A routine was quickly established, and it would repeat itself for the next five days. When it came time to shoot something, the porters would hand Berg the gear, he'd set-up and shoot, and then hand it all back to them. Lepik, who toted the tripod and a large backpack during the first part of the day, also relinquished the extra weight.

"I'll be handing some of this off to the porters," he

said. "A 10, 12, 14 percent grade with all this stuff is no easy task. There will definitely be some strategic reduction going on." Eventually, all of us westerners would end up carrying just our smaller backpacks and water supplies.

The warmth at this altitude, just three degrees of latitude south of the equator, would last only as long as the sun was shining. When the sun went down, the heat quickly dissipated. Equator or no equator, at 9,000 feet, darkness means coldness. I realized this when I popped out of the tent to take a leak on night one. I also realized something else.

"Holy Moly, Brender," I said to my tent-mate. "Check this out!"

From horizon to horizon, in all directions, with no light pollution to speak of, we saw stars, stars, and more stars — like, every star ever created. On ensuing nights, with even less vegetation around, it became even more phenomenal. I had seen otherworldly views previously in Alaska and other places way up north, but nothing like this.

We were small.

On day two, we arose to what became a standard daily breakfast: porridge with honey, toast, a fried egg, and a piece of sausage. Conversation was still a bit tentative. The group was still new to one another, and we could all sense a bit of apprehension for what lay ahead. Berg and Lepik chatted about their equipment. Then we learned of some early symptoms of altitude illness.

A couple of the fellas felt dizzy overnight, while one or two experienced headaches briefly. I was surprised to hear it, especially from the super-human Bruins captain, because I didn't suffer from these symptoms at all. I just couldn't sleep. I slept for maybe two hours the first night.

"You guys ready for this?" Chára asked as we finished eating. "Just seven hours today." He smiled.

We washed down breakfast with a cup of tea, rolled up our sleeping bags, and prepared to head out. We grabbed our daypacks, and, not unlike James Earl Jones disappearing into the cornfield in *Field of Dreams*, we walked single-file behind our guide, Aloyce, into a gap in the surrounding tall brush. The campsite vanished immediately behind us. The first of two three-and-a-half-hour treks was underway.

The porters would stay behind, pack up, and carry everything to the next campsite. It was a daily ritual: an hour or two into each hike, sixteen porters would catch up to us, pass us, and move on ahead to the next overnight location. We marvelled at the ability of each guy to carry forty pounds of gear, barefoot or wearing second-hand shoes at best, while hopping over rocks and ruts and moving at three times our speed. The five Africans who stayed with us the entire time were Aloyce, his assistant head guide, and the three porters carrying the TV equipment.

"They're in excellent shape," Chára said, awed. This from the man considered to be the NHL's fitness maniac, with a six-foot-nine inch frame, less than 10 percent body fat on his 255 pounds, and a legendary work ethic. "These guys are carrying thirty-, forty-, fifty-pound loads on their heads. Look, *on their heads*. Incredible shape. Obviously we wouldn't be able to do this without them, so all the credit goes to them."

The first half of our day involved a relatively vigorous uphill hike through rocks, along thinning brush, and across little volcanic valleys running downhill from the mountain peaks. At one point we stopped at a cave, which had been used as shelter by various peoples over the millennia, and took photographs and video. Aloyce pointed to the hoof and paw prints of the local fauna that had passed through.

"Dik-diks come in here and chew," he said.

"Any snakes?" Brender asked.

"Anything that can eat us?" Chára volleyed.

Much to the relief of his wary charges, Aloyce pointed out that no deadly snakes or animals would be passing along at this altitude on this side of the mountain.

Throughout the day, we'd stop and allow Berg to get shots he needed for the documentary. Naturally, the focus was on Chára and his trek; the rest of us were the supporting cast. Needless to say, the visuals were impressive; Berg had an incredible natural environment in which to work.

"We've passed 11,500 feet," Chára pointed out as we neared the end of the morning portion of the day's climb.

My footwear choices were backwards the first two days. Due to the dustiness of the trail on day one, I should have worn the hiking boots. Instead, I wore and trashed my running shoes. Day two, the shoes would have been perfect, with less dust, a solid trail, and a relatively rock-free environment. I went with the rental boots, and thus developed my first of many blisters.

After four hours, we stopped for lunch. Kibo, the snow-capped volcano of Kilimanjaro, loomed straight ahead of us.

"You can almost reach out and grab it," I said to Chára.

Our group started to bond. We really began to appreciate the experience we were sharing. We laughed about the fatigue and marvelled at the porters and the scenery. I also began to get to know the Bruins captain a lot better. As the TV beat reporter for NESN in Boston for the past three seasons, I travelled with the team, but I always kept my distance from "Big Z" and the other players, as part of protocol. Sure, we'd have fun on various feature shoots and such, but for the most part, I very rarely socialized with the hockey players.

On this trip, I gradually learned about Chára's sensitivities, particularly for those less fortunate, especially children. Also, he is far more intelligent than most athletes (he speaks six languages), and, despite his bear-like size, his fitness level, and his on-ice demeanour, he was, simply, a very nice guy. We'd eventually talk off the record about Bruins personnel, as in what players were keepers and who would have to be replaced before a championship was realistic.

"If you repeat any of this, Simmer, I will kill you," he said, smiling. "No, seriously," he'd add a few steps later.

After lunch, we turned left and levelled out. Most of the day's ascent, 3,200 feet, had been accomplished. We hiked at just below 12,000 feet for the next three hours toward the Mawenzi crater. We were angling our way south along the east side of Kibo, gradually acclimatizing, and gradually moving toward our position for summit day. By the time we finished this flatter, rockier portion of the trip, Kibo was actually farther off to our right, and we were still three to four hours from Mawenzi in the distance.

"I don't want to get too far ahead of myself," Chára told the TV camera. "I'm thinking one day at a time, take care of business every day. Make sure that you eat right, drink enough fluids, that you don't go too fast, and [that you] get enough rest."

Night two camp was set up on a hillside under some huge, barren trees, near a stream that ran to an area of caves called Kikelewa. A pair of large black ravens perched nearby, keeping watch.

We ate, sat, and chatted in the dinner tent until dusk. No cell phones, no internet, just the group, just conversation.

Chára felt a bit lightheaded and exhausted. Berg, Lepik, and Brender had varying degrees of dizziness and headache. Me: I just couldn't sleep.

I began my nightly custom. At dusk, I'd remove my socks, and with Brender's pocket knife I'd slice open the two or three blisters on each foot. After dabbing away the bloody, copper-coloured fluid, I'd touch-up each spot with an alcohol wipe Chára had provided from his medical kit.

Then I'd strip down, climb into the sleeping bag, and try to doze off. Without a mat beneath me, I'd feel every single pebble or stone through the floor of the tent and the sheer layer of my sleeping bag. When lying on my side, my weight created a form of hip pointer. The bone was aggravated, and I couldn't stop rolling back and forth.

On this second night, after tossing and turning and repositioning and listening to Brender snore for a couple of hours, I couldn't take it anymore. I began to wonder if I'd ever sleep again.

"Shit!" I yelled at the top of my lungs. "Son of a bitch!"
No one heard me.

———————————

Our start to the climb on YouTube: Summer with Zee: Climbing Kilimanjaro Part 1

"For sure, one of the toughest things, if not the toughest thing, in my life, that I've done."

Boston Bruins Captain Zdeno Chára,
after six days on Kilimanjaro

BIG Z ON THE MOUNTAIN Part 2

After night two on Kilimanjaro, I had slept a grand total of about three hours. Not a good formula when you're trekking four to seven hours a day at altitude. I was becoming legitimately concerned about how this fatigue might affect my way to the top, and I wasn't the only one. Producer Darryl Lepik was also complaining of sleep issues. The other climbers were suffering from general fatigue, mild dizziness, and headaches, the details and extent of which they didn't share.

Overcoming the challenges and symptoms was made easier by being immersed in the incredible natural surroundings. On day three, we added another 2,400 feet of altitude. We crisscrossed a number of streams and volcanic valleys as we worked our way to Mawenzi. We saw dik-dik antelope running on a hillside, encountered a handful of birds, stumbled across a lizard or two, and were constantly surrounded by bees.

The environment became drier and more desolate as we continued up, and the scenery became more surreal and dramatic, with the ominous presence of mountain peaks on either side of us. When we stopped for a water break, we'd look back down the slope of the mountain, above the clouds that surrounded Kilimanjaro. The view was awe inspiring, but also eerily isolating.

Our straightforward and vigorous four-hour trek brought us to the Mawenzi crater at 14,200 feet. We lunched here, took an afternoon acclimatization hike up and down a ridge, and then camped here as well. This hike was more of a rock climb, our most perilous of the entire trip, requiring the use of all four limbs. The ridges of the crater were made up of strewn, jagged volcanic rock. We switch-backed up the lower portion and then pulled ourselves up the rocks along the western rim. Before returning to the crater floor, we sat on this rocky perch for about a half-hour. Looking out across the "saddle" at Kibo — the prize, the roof of Africa, the summit of Kilimanjaro — we truly began to ponder the task that lay ahead.

"It's been pretty tough at times, but the toughest is yet to come," Mark Brender said.

"I'm trying not to think about it yet," Chára said. "We're just sitting there trying to get used to the altitude. Looking out at Kilimanjaro sitting in front of you, it doesn't get any better than that. Just sitting there and relaxing; those are priceless moments."

Summit day (or night) was about thirty-three hours away.

The trek up the ridge provided magnificent scenery, an exciting and adrenaline-filled climb, and another 700 feet or so of acclimatization. Aloyce had maximized our preparation to avoid altitude illness, and he led us around the landscape to some amazing spots. Each night, there were fewer and fewer "other climbers" on our path. The first camp had a handful of groups, the second night maybe three or four, and on night three, beneath the spires of Mawenzi, it was just us and one other small group.

Compared to this spot, beside a small pond on the floor of a volcanic crater a couple of miles high in Tanzania, it was hard to imagine a more dramatic campsite.

"This has been amazing," Darryl Lepik said as he spoke into my handheld camera. "Just the scenery and the experience, it's been absolutely phenomenal, and I expect that to continue for a couple days."

Lepik's occasional nickname during this trip was "lip balm," because he seemed to be the only guy who remembered to pack it. Brender had some ChapStick, but not much, and who wants to share that? Lepik had a small jar of the stuff, and I was like a junkie. I didn't want to push my luck by asking too often, but at the end of each day, begging for balm became mandatory. At one point on day three, I thought my upper lip had shriveled off my face.

Things were looking up by day four, in more ways than one. I managed about three hours of sleep overnight and most of the next hike was relatively flat.

It was time to cross the saddle: the seven-mile plateau ridge between Mawenzi and the base of our ultimate destination. Ten minutes into the hike, we had wound out of the Mawenzi bowl, crossed a small ridge, and just like that, it was as if the previous night's camp didn't exist. It was gone; the isolated landscape had disappeared from sight.

As discussed by the group at the previous night's dinner in the mess tent, that night-three campsite would be our last "normal" campsite. Each morning, we had enjoyed the routine of waking up, eating breakfast together and discussing the day ahead, venturing out, reaching a camp, settling in, relaxing, exploring, eating dinner, and then turning in when the sun went down. That would all change on night four. It would be a night awake on the mountain.

The trek across took us exactly five hours, gradually leaving Mawenzi in our past and drawing Kibo imminently into our future.

"That was a pretty nice hike," Chára said. "Nothing too hard, it was almost relaxing as we get used to the climate and altitude. I tried not to think of the summit too much, but it was tough because you're staring right up at it."

We arrived at what our guide, Aloyce, called the "School Camp," base camp, off the beaten track of the main path at 15,400 feet. It was a spot that was established and previously used by the organization Outward Bound. We were the only trekking party at the site. Instead of putting us with potentially a half-dozen other trekking groups at the Kibo Hut on the main trail to the west, Aloyce allowed us some privacy and an exclusive view of the surroundings.

It was at base camp that I came to another realization: I hadn't taken a dump for four days, since before the entire journey started. Nor had Chára apparently. When I weaved my way through some boulders just to the west of our campsite to find the "outhouse," I was surprised to find Zdeno had beaten me there. Three little steps led up to a four foot-by-four foot piece of wood with a football-sized hole cut out of the middle — this was the floor of the outhouse. There was no door or wall on the front, just three short tin walls on the sides and back, and a four-by-four foot tin roof above. The walls and roof were rattling in the wind. The act of crapping involved target practice and squatting over the hole like a baseball catcher while looking out over the grandeur.

Upon seeing Chára, I turned back around and said, "Oh, hey, I guess I'll wait 'til I see you come back to camp. Nice form."

He wasn't smiling, but I don't think he heard me. A new term popped into my head: human giraffe yoga excretion.

Base camp was very windy and wicked cold, even in the daylight. Such is life at 15,000 feet above sea level. There was nothing to do but to bundle up, eat quickly, and wait for the sun to go down. There was plenty of nervous energy in the mess tent. Aloyce sat in and briefed us on what was going to take place.

The plan was to try to get a little sleep starting at seven p.m. before gathering outside again at eleven p.m. for a quick snack and departure. We'd leave for the summit before midnight.

Why midnight? Because the climb to the crater rim of Kibo took six hours. After arriving there at sunrise, the trip to Uhuru, the mountain's highest point, was another three-hour round trip. After that, a three-hour descent to Kibo Hut on the main trail, followed by three and a half more hours to the next overnight campsite. For those who went the distance, it was a sixteen-hour trek.

Our climb to the summit would first involve working diagonally westward and up, to join the main trail well above Kibo Hut, and then to finish like most everyone else, at Gilman's Point straight up the mountain. Gilman's Point sits at 18,650 feet.

During the last few minutes of daylight, my fellow trekkers offered up some extra layers for me to wear, another pair of socks, and a few extra Band-Aids.

We enjoyed one last mountain sunset, with a view back to Mawenzi across the saddle, and a view down through the clouds to some faraway village lights on the East African plain.

When the sun sank, the temperature went with it. We wore three layers to bed, two pairs of socks, and a toque. I would add a third pair of socks before leaving, not so much for the cold, but to ease and prevent blisters.

By dark, we had packed up the materials we wouldn't be taking up, and left them aside for the porters to carry to the next campsite. We laid our last layers next to us in the tents, along with our headlamps.

There was no chance in hell I'd be able to sleep.

After squirming around for what seemed like four hours, I heard Brender awake and asked him what time it was, expecting and hoping to hear something close to eleven o'clock.

"Five to nine," he said, much to my disappointment. We had two more hours to kill, and I surprised myself by actually nodding off for half an hour. Apparently nervous anticipation can be exhausting.

Day five for us on Kilimanjaro officially began a few minutes before midnight. When I popped out of my tent with all of my gear in place, all of my layers heaped on, and my headlamp functioning, the rest of the group was already standing by.

It was pitch black. We had a dramatic panorama of stars overhead, but no one really noticed. With our headlamps on and our focus entirely upon the ground in front of us, we didn't care a whole lot for the stars.

For the next six hours, we'd be climbing in the dark. Vertically, we had about 3,200 feet to gain. Slowly: *pole, pole*.

"Kind of like the anticipation before a big game," Chára described. "Really nervous, cold hands, cold feet, getting ready to basically start the walk."

Aloyce, the head guide, led the way out of camp. I was next for no particular reason, then Big Z, then Darryl, then Bergy, then Brender, then the three porters carrying the TV equipment, and then the assistant head guide.

The journey redefined "patience is a virtue." We literally walked with our lamps shining down upon the set of feet in front of us and took something slightly larger than baby steps for six hours. Each of us had a spiked walking pole in one hand to help with balance. Occasionally we had to navigate our way along ledges, around boulders, and over rock outcroppings, but most of the time we trudged upward through scree (loose rock). The talus gave way a little bit with almost every step, and each of us would periodically slip to a knee or almost fall over when the rocks shifted under our feet.

There was no talk other than to ask about each other's well-being during water breaks, of which there were many. Despite the fact that the landscape within the range of our headlamps was fascinating and ever changing, the stepping and trudging became monotonous at times, almost trance inducing.

At one point, after I almost clipped Bergy with the follow-through of my walking stick, I said, "Sorry, you alright?"

"Shut up and walk," he answered. We were all feeling a certain level of disbelief and frustration at the progress. What I didn't realize was that the others were also experiencing annoying, maybe even painful, levels of altitude symptoms. I wouldn't know until hours later who was completely worn out already, who had a wicked headache, or who was ready to quit.

Mark Brender, who would later experience extreme disorientation symptoms on the crater rim, was actually at this point the spunkiest. He offered enthusiastic words of encouragement at every stop.

After two or three rests, we changed up the order. Chára went immediately behind Aloyce. The big man had some trouble with his footing and found the going tough. He explained later that the slipping and sliding on the scree dramatically added to his fatigue.

On one hand, the pace tested everyone's patience; frustration stemmed from often having to halt due to the man in front of you slipping. At other times, when a rhythm was established, left-right, left-right, crunch-crunch, crunch-crunch, the climb was almost soothing. Those stretches didn't last long.

About three hours in, we came across another line of headlamps to our left. Another group was making its way up to the summit via the main path. A few minutes later, we'd merge onto that path just behind them. Soon after the merge, we took another rest.

"It's the most difficult thing I've ever done," said Chára later. "I've done a lot of hard training, many kinds, but nothing compares. You're baby stepping behind one another, climbing, zigzagging, losing balance. It's dark, you're tired, and your feet are slipping on loose gravel. We must have stopped to rest fifteen times."

An indelible image for all of us was the view from the main trail towards the top of the mountain in the dark. At various points above us, you could see the random and rare light from distant headlamps. The same below us: distant specks of light, in lines, creeping, turning this way and that, making their way up the mountain.

We also stared towards where we thought the sky met the top of the mountain. It still seemed a long way off, and we already felt like we had marched for an eternity.

A few minutes after we gained the main trail, we came across a little plateau where a group of trekkers were resting.

"We're halfway to Gilman's Point," Aloyce informed us.

"Halfway!?"

"Holy shit, you're kidding me!"

"Oh my God."

We had three hours of climbing to go, working with a mental cocktail of fatigue and altitude sickness.

"Suck it up, boys. Let's go."

The next three hours consisted of climbing a switch-back trail made up almost exclusively of loose rock. We dug in, and after a handful of water breaks, some team building words of encouragement, and some timely "*pole, poles*" thrown in, we finally arrived at Gilman's Point. The last two hundred yards were excruciating on mind and body; the Point kept disappearing and reappearing as we wound and climbed our way through a labyrinth of rocks and boulders.

A few minutes after sunrise on July 4, 2008, we gathered at 18,650 feet.

A snow-filled crater sat a few hundred feet below us within the vast volcanic bowl of Kilimanjaro. Huge glaciers towered in the distance to the east and closer to us on the west side of the summit. Also off to the left, a narrow path up the ridge of ice and lava rock stretched out before us. It ran along the crater rim another kilometre and another 800 feet above us up to Uhuru Point, the highest point in Africa, an hour and a half hike from where we stood.

We took a few minutes at Gilman's Point to celebrate and photograph our accomplishment. Out came the video cameras, and then out came the question.

"Who's going on to Uhuru?" Brender asked. "Are you going on to Uhuru?"

"Yes," I said. "There's no chance in hell I'm not going at this point."

I believe the small doses of Diamox anti-altitude-illness medication had helped me. I was exhausted but had no symptoms and felt determined. The others hadn't taken it. I was disappointed to hear Chára and Lepik say they weren't going.

"Too tired," said Chára. "[I'm] exhausted. Completely out of energy." He didn't want to risk injury from fatigue.

Berg and Brender decided to give it a go. The three of us, along with Aloyce, his assistant, and three TV porters all began the trek up the trail.

A few minutes in, Brender had a change of heart.

"I'm gonna go back," he said. Unfortunately for him, when he returned to Gilman's Point, Chára and Lepik had already left to head back down the main trail. Unsure exactly where to go, particularly without a porter, Brender decided to wait two and a half hours for us to return. Not a good decision.

Meanwhile, Berg got a little goofy about halfway up the Uhuru trail. He doubted his ability to finish off the trip and was getting dizzy. Aside from us coaxing him, two other factors pushed him to the top. One was walking behind Aloyce step by step while they both held on to Aloyce's walking stick horizontally. He was being towed, essentially. The other motivation and inspiration came from a passerby who was headed down from the top.

"If there are any Americans here, happy Fourth of July," the young lady said.

Although I don't consider myself particularly patriotic, the words provided a definite boost for me as well. It was cool our endeavor to the mountaintop occurred on such a significant date.

Damn right, I was thinking. *Let's celebrate a holiday on the top of Africa.*

The path became snowy, icy, and slick the higher we moved. We picked and weaved our way to 19,350 feet. Out came the video cameras.

Me, a porter, head guide Aloyce, Mark Berg, and another porter at Uhuru Peak, the highest point in Africa.

"I can't believe we made it," Berg said with a big smile.

"We're here," I said on camera, pointing to the wooden signage at the peak.

After ten minutes or so: Done. I could not wait to get off the top of that freaking mountain.

We hustled as best we could back along the narrow crater path. Only twice were there spots where you had to be extra careful. A wrong step would mean falling hundreds of feet into the bowl. We arrived back at Gilman's Point to find a zombie named Mark Brender.

Sitting at above 18,000 feet for almost three hours had turned Brender into one big massive headache. He couldn't think, he couldn't see straight, and he could hardly move.

Aloyce and I guided him down through the boulders

and rocks near the top, and then Aloyce alone handled Brender the rest of the way down through the scree to Kibo Hut. Berg and I "skied" our way down through the loose rock.

At one point, a descending teenager above us somehow jarred loose a large rock that came thundering down the mountain towards me.

"Slider!" someone yelled. It missed my head by about two arm lengths and then missed a girl who was descending twenty yards below me by about six feet. Two or three times the size of a bowling ball and moving about twenty-five miles an hour, the rock would have killed one of us had we been hit. If it hadn't mangled one of us immediately, it would have meant slow death by internal injury. There's no MedEvac off Kilimanjaro.

For a few moments, I stared up at the kid and was ready to beat the shit out of him, but logic and fatigue almost immediately took over. Despite the near-death experience, I was mostly focused on "get me off this mountain." Satisfying my anger would have meant walking back up.

For three hours we leapt, jogged, and slid down through the rocks to Kibo Hut, where Lepik and Chára had been waiting for hours. After swapping medical stories and tales from the top, we came to the realization that we still had another three hours to go. Fortunately, it was all downhill or flat to the next campsite, but still, we couldn't believe we had three more hours of hiking. It had been twelve hours since the "day" began.

It was hot, it was dry, and for the only time in my life, I felt like I was actually sleeping as I walked. I couldn't keep my eyes open. Chára, Lepik, and Berg marched on ahead with a porter. Brender, Aloyce, and I lagged behind. At one point during a water break, I almost zonked out sitting on a bench. We peeled off layers as we went down through 14,000 feet.

By five thirty p.m., we arrived at Horombo Camp, a crowded and boisterous area along the main trail. With the descent, Lepik's and Brender's altitude symptoms fortunately subsided. I skipped dinner, sliced my blisters, and passed out. Dead to the world, I missed the sounds the others heard a few hours after dusk.

"Simba!" the Africans said. A lion had passed within a hundred yards of our tents, grunting in the darkness. The next day, we'd see its enormous paw prints on the trail.

Our final day involved six more hours of downhill trekking. Berg and I, the two oldest guys in the group, the two who had pushed to Uhuru on day five, were, not surprisingly, aching the most on day six. My feet were killing me, and Bergy had a legitimate hitch in his giddy-up.

"My knees are sore," he said.

His limp spurred John Wayne comparisons. He walked like he had just hopped off his horse and was about to enter a saloon.

During the first part of the day, we strode through dry moorland and later crossed footbridges over small stream-clad valleys. Early in the day, there was actually a dusting of snow on a few of them. The second half of the hike, we descended through rainforest.

In fact, according to the locals, over the course of the previous twenty-four hours, we had travelled through every climate on Earth: glacial ice at the summit, all the way down through rainforest at the bottom of the journey.

At one point along the trail, we observed black monkeys jumping around in the trees just above us. Aloyce had no other name for them, just "black." They were very active, leaping over our heads from tree to tree and walking and eating very near to us at ground level. Cousins, if you will, of humans, they stared back at us like little kids, casually chewing on leaves and swinging around with the help of long opposable thumbs.

Further along, we walked beneath black-and-white colobus monkeys sitting in the canopy. They were much less active than their all-black relatives.

As we neared the national park gate and the village of Marangu, we came across small children, and later women, who came up from the village to beg. A German couple walking ahead of me stopped and gave a boy a dollar for a flower he had picked. The other locals simply asked for money, clothes, or whatever we could spare.

It was quite a reality check after being alone on the mountain.

Once we took the final few steps and were back at the national park gate, we bid farewell to the porters. We tipped them more generously than they were accustomed to. They applauded enthusiastically when Aloyce read out the gratuity amounts. He, his assistant, the cook, and the three porters who toted the TV gear earned extra. Among the twenty of them, they split about $800. We also gave them our boots, as is customary, and much of our gear and clothing. Chára gave away practically everything he had taken up on the mountain.

"These people can use everything they can get, and if I had more stuff, I'd give that to them as well," Zdeno stated.

Bergy, Lepik, and Brender were generous as well. I couldn't help out, unfortunately, as I had to return my rental clothes instead of give them away.

We bid the porters and Aloyce farewell, jumped into a Land Rover, and headed out through the gate, through the village of Marangu, toward the lodge.

There was a sense of relief, satisfaction, and sadness as we bid adieu to a group of men we'd never see again. Their faces were unforgettable, forever tied to our once-in-a-lifetime trek upon the great Kilimanjaro, an adventure that soon after it ended seemed more like a dream than reality.

We understood Chára rarely, if ever, drank. However, that night he and the rest of us gathered for a couple of beers at the lodge to reminisce.

When we started the trip, we saw Chára as an enormous, mean-looking, media-weary, fitness machine. By the end, he was a friendly, smart, sensitive world traveller. Image *isn't* everything.

For him, I went from being the tall TV guy who travelled with the team from the media he disliked to a sportscaster guy he could trust with information, who appreciated many of the same things in life as he did, and who had just summited a mountain.

Chára was appreciative of the camaraderie and the time spent, and he expressed little regret for tiring before the summit. On a Kilimanjaro postcard I asked him to autograph for my son, he wrote, "Hi Ian, your dad was the strongest of all of us. We had an unforgettable life experience. Your friend, Zdeno Chára, No. 33."

Zdeno Chára still plays for the Bruins. The team won a Stanley Cup in 2011. He'll be an unrestricted free agent in the summer of 2018 at the age of forty-one.

Darryl Lepik left the NHL in 2009 and has been working in marketing and production in both New York City and Colorado.

Mark Berg, a thirty-year veteran of the production business, lives in metropolitan Detroit and is the owner of Great Lakes Teleproductions Inc. I last ran into him while covering the last ever Red Wings game at the Joe Louis Arena in April 2017.

Higher up the mountain: Summer with Zee: Climbing Kilimanjaro Part 2

Reaching the summit, search: Simmer Hockey Odyssey Kili'

"Shot! Blocked down out to centre
by Zetterberg . . . four seconds and
three . . . the Gold goes to Sweden!"

Mike "Doc" Emrick's call of the final seconds
of 2006 Olympic Gold Medal Game

THE ITALIAN JOB

For four weeks in the winter of 2006, I spent my time in just five places in Torino, Italy. Aside from a quick side trip to Venice, I spent the entire pre-Olympic and Olympic experience in the "Detroit of Italy," the home of much of the country's auto industry. The five places included the Riberi Media Village where I slept a bit, drank late, and ate bad breakfasts; the Olympic media center where I ate other meals and schmoozed in the NBC commissary; the big rink (Palasport Olimpico), with the funky see-through seats; the Esposizioni (Espo-SEATS-zee-oh-nee) rink, which seemed thirty years older than it actually was;

and the always festive Zelli's wine bar, where I watched *Today Show* host Katie Couric dance on a table. She wasn't the only one.

During the regular hockey season of 2005–06, I was an on-air TV guy in Boston, covering the Bruins for the New England Sports Network (NESN), but for the duration of the Torino Olympic Winter Games, I was the staff hockey researcher for NBC Sports. For the first time ever, the network was televising every men's and women's hockey game, regardless of match-up. Since there were so many games for the play-by-play announcers and colour analysts to do, and only so much time to prepare for all of them, I helped them with some of their research and preparation.

This meant going back and forth between the rinks

Our entire NBC Olympic hockey crew, minus me, who was at the practice rink getting notes about Team Sweden.

pretty much all day, every day. For example, if Mike "Doc" Emrick and John Davidson were calling the Sweden–USA women's semi-final game in one time slot but had the Slovakia–USA men's game the next day, I'd be at the Slovakia practice taking notes and getting updates to pass along. If Kenny Albert and Peter McNab were calling Sweden–Russia men's on Wednesday and needed info on Canada for Friday, I'd be freezing my ass off at one of the coldest practice rinks on the planet, getting injury updates and writing down quotes from Team Canada.

Fun stuff, eh? Damn right. It meant being helpful in hockey utopia, and with a dozen years of play-by-play experience, I knew to jot down what wouldn't get in the official game notes.

During the day, this job was all-consuming. So much

so, in fact, that I'm the only person (I think) missing from the massive NBC hockey staff photograph taken in the stands at the big rink midway through the Games. I vaguely remember seeing the notice on the food tent by the production trucks, "Hockey production team photo, everyone, 2:00 p.m., Palasport." *That couldn't possibly include me*, I thought. So while producers Gord Cutler and Carlos DeMolina and eighty-three other people on the hockey production staff were getting their picture taken, I was at the Team Sweden men's practice, talking to Fredrik Modin about his groin.

When I saw the photo at the end of the Games, I was initially kind of bummed, but let's face it, I have all the pictures of me I'll ever need; now I had a photo of all the people I worked with at my first (and maybe only) Olympics.

The practice rink was attached to the Espo' rink, but getting to it involved a long walk outside around the building. The stands were freezing, like hard-to-write, hard-to-even-move-your-fingers type cold. Limited access meant grabbing players as they walked to the bus in a cordoned-off area, which made the experience even more bothersome.

I preferred going to the actual event rinks for rare morning skates. Once, practically by myself in the stands early in the Games, I watched Jaromír Jágr and half of the Czech men's team play a game of four-on-four shinny inside the blueline before their first practice. The skill, the movement, the dangling were breathtaking: smile-out-loud entertainment.

Interviews after practice and more formally after games

at the Espo' and at Palasport took place in an area called the "mixed zone." This is standard operating procedure at the Olympic Games and at International Ice Hockey Federation events. The players leave the ice and, before they get to their dressing room, have to walk down a long corridor of sorts, with a wall on one side and a flimsy rope or short fence on the other, separating the players from the throng of media. The luxuries of hiding after a bad game or ducking out a side door to avoid a writer or TV cameras — moves made by more than a few NHL players during the regular season — aren't allowed here. Blowing off the media at the Olympics meant having to walk with your head down, running the gauntlet of the mixed zone past a couple hundred reporters and cameras, for all to see. It happened very rarely. Players always stopped and at least talked in their native tongue to reporters from their home country.

As the Games moved along, it was rather evident this wasn't going to be Canada's or the USA's year in the marquee event, men's ice hockey. Canada took care of business early on, winning their first two preliminary-round games against host Italy 7–2 and Germany 5–1.

But after a day off, Team Canada got tripped up. The Swiss, behind Carolina Hurricanes goalie Martin Gerber's forty-nine saves, shut out the Canadians 2–0 at the Esposizioni. Paul DiPietro was the other hero, scoring both goals for Switzerland, his second on a two-man advantage in the second period. That was it. Head coach Ralph Krueger smiled on the Swiss bench, his team winning with only eighteen shots on goal. It was pretty simple: Gerber had stood on his head.

Canada responded by losing to Finland the very next day by the exact same score. Instead of Martin Brodeur in net, it was Roberto Luongo who took the loss. The Finns beating Canada wasn't exactly a surprise. Teemu Selänne, who finished as the tournament's leading scorer, and Saku Koivu, who finished second, took advantage of their team's speed on the big ice to frustrate the Canadians. Selänne had the game winner in the first.

Canada, who chose not to name eighteen-year-old NHL rookie Sidney Crosby to the roster, finished the prelims by beating the Czech Republic 3–2, enough to earn them the third seed entering the win-or-go-home quarterfinals.

This, in any Olympic tournament, is when the nail biting begins. The pools cross over for the quarters, meaning seed one from Group A plays seed four from Group B, A2 vs. B3, A3 vs. B2, and A4 vs. B1.

In what was the coolest environment of the men's tourney, outside of the Finland versus Sweden final, the Russians and the Canadians faced off on February 22, 2006, at the Esposizioni, for bragging rights in their long-time rivalry and the chance to move on.

The Espo was rocking an intimate but very noisy sea of red. I sat in the stands with former Team USA women's star and future Hockey Hall of Famer–turned broadcaster Cammi Granato, just above NBC's broadcast position, about fifty feet above centre ice. It was an expansive, makeshift media section. She was one of the analysts for the women's games, having been surprisingly, controversially, left off the USA roster that year. We did our own off-air analysis of the men's games and laughed our butts off as her husband, Ray Ferraro, sat in front of us doing the actual commentary.

The Russia–Canada game was intense, as the teams traded chances but remained scoreless into the third period. It was just ninety seconds into that final stanza, with Canada's Todd Bertuzzi off for interference, that Alexander Ovechkin streaked down the wing from our left to right and unloaded a slapper that beat Brodeur inside the far post for what would be the game winner. Half of the red sea leapt to its feet; the other half went quiet.

Canada failed to tie it on three consecutive power plays and gave up a meaningless goal to Russia with twenty-three seconds remaining. The final minute of their effort had completely deteriorated into frustration and chippy-ness. They lost 2–0 for the third time at the Olympics. Party over.

The Americans weren't nearly as interesting. It was a classic case of not getting over the hump. They just didn't have it. They were obviously paying too much attention to the travelling contingent of hot blonde hockey fans from Riga, sitting just above the glass in the right-wing corner, when they tied the Latvians 3–3 to open the Games on February 15. The next day, they beat Kazakhstan 4–1, before losing three consecutive one-goal games to Slovakia, Sweden, and Russia.

In the group-crossover quarterfinal do-or-die against Finland, the Americans actually made a game of it, tying it 2–2 early in the second after falling behind. But one never got the feeling the score was legitimate or the effort sincere. Olli Jokinen scored twice in the third period, the Yanks scored late to make it somewhat compelling, but Finland moved on 4–3.

It may have been the subconscious lack of confidence in goaltending that did Team USA in. Rick DiPietro, who wasn't exactly sterling in their final loss, was the main man. The backups were Robert Esche and John Grahame. The trio didn't exactly instill a world-beater sense of invincibility.

Officially, Canada finished the Games in seventh place, the USA in eighth. Their early exits from the hockey tournament led to their next challenge: finding flights home. And it was every man for himself. Flights had all been booked for a later date, with a medal-round appearance being somewhat presumed. Instead, the two teams drank together at expat bars while awaiting their new transportation arrangements. I remember running into USA extra defenceman Hal Gill, then a Bruin, and his wife at an ATM across the street from Murphy's, a popular Irish pub.

"Trying to get outta here," said "Skillsie." Many of the North American players were hoping to put the Games behind them as quickly as possible, and returning home early would mean a chance to skate with their NHL teammates who weren't at the Olympics. Formal NHL practices started back up a few days before the medal round wrapped up in Italy.

There were other Bruins participating at the Olympics in Torino. I found rookie defenceman Milan Jurcina entertaining. "Jerky" was an amiable kid, who attempted to use his size and competitiveness to overcome shortcomings in skating and skill. He became a regular on the blueline for Slovakia at international events.

Marco Sturm would have represented Germany, but he was suffering through the first of many knee injuries that would eventually limit the latter portion of his NHL career. He finished with 273 points in 556 games played in an NHL career that ended in 2012.

––––––––––––––

Recent Bruin–turned–San Jose Shark Joe Thornton drew plenty of interest at the Olympics as well. Despite the general media frenzy around Thornton and his high-profile trade, I didn't pay that much attention. Not a big fan of his overall demeanour towards winning and losing during our brief time together in Beantown, and a strong proponent of "The Joe Thornton Trade," I didn't really follow or approach "Jumbo" during his mixed-zone visits. I think I grabbed some audio from him on only one occasion at the Games.

Less than three months had passed since his trade had rocked the hockey world. I went into the Bruins dressing room post-game, as I always did, the night of November 29, 2005, in New Jersey. Thornton had lost a defensive zone draw to Devils centre John Madden in the final minute of regulation. Madden won the puck cleanly, flipped it over to Alexander Mogilny, who ripped a shot past Boston goalie Andrew Raycroft for the game winner. The Bruins had blown a 2–0 lead and now had a three-game losing streak. They had lost nine of ten, having just recently ended a six-game losing streak in Toronto.

I'll never forget the interview Thornton did with two writers and myself after the loss, and this after getting burned on the face-off. We were crammed just inside the visitors dressing room door, and somewhat rushed, as the team hastily prepped for the post-game charter flight home.

"We're fine, we'll be okay," Thornton repeated. I knew some surfer dudes from living in Hawaii for five years, but the hockey man in me, and the hockey reporter in me, watching this team flail in the early season, didn't appreciate the beachy response. Dude, you're not fine.

Yes, as captain, he was generally always willing to talk post game, which is commendable, but the mantra was far too routine, far too casual, and never laced with urgency. After the loss to the Devils, his response seemed unfathomable to me.

The next night, a Wednesday, I was out with my assistant, Abby, at The Druid pub in Cambridge, Massachusetts, down the street from where I lived that season. NESN showed up on my caller ID.

"Uh oh, what the heck is this?"

I stepped outside the noisy bar to hear *SportsDesk* coordinating producer Rob Wallace's voice on the other end of the line.

"Simmer, where are you?" he asked.

"In Cambridge. What's going on?"

"The Bruins just traded Joe Thornton," he declared.

It really happens: my jaw actually dropped.

"Can you come in?"

Uh oh. I was conflicted. Of course I was interested in the opportunity to jump on *SportsDesk* live with anchor Hazel Mae to handle this gigantic sports story. But I was also two or three glasses of wine deep. I was buzzed, and, besides, I wasn't really confident I could bring any significant historical perspective to Thornton's tenure in Boston. I was only twenty-six games into my first season with the Bruins. I weighed the benefits and the potential pratfalls of going on the air or not going on the air, and made the right decision. I'd been around the business long enough to know that the factors working against me, especially the wine buzz, could do great harm to my career, while the potential downside of not going on the air that night hardly existed. My decision was made even easier knowing that NESN had the option of calling on Kevin Paul Dupont, Hockey-Hall-of-Fame-honoured writer for the *Boston Globe*, as an analyst to break things down.

I loved the trade from the get-go and was clearly in the minority when I said so. From the perspective of leadership and chemistry, I felt the Bruins had been treading water. They needed what some refer to as a change in culture. Thornton could pile up points all he wanted, but the Bruins would never win a Cup with him as captain. And they didn't. Boston General Manager Mike O'Connell traded Jumbo to the Sharks for speedy German winger Marco Sturm, stalwart defenceman Brad Stuart, and a third-line centre, Wayne Primeau. The fans went nuts, the reporters who behaved like fans went nuts, but to many in the hockey world, the reasoning was clear.

"O.C.," as O'Connell was known, went through hell. The Boston fans ripped him and chanted for his dismissal at games. The former first overall pick in the 1997 Draft, Thornton was one of those "homegrown" Bruins that Boston hockey fans loved. They felt betrayed. Making it worse, Thornton went on to win the Hart Trophy as league Most Valuable Player in 2006, the first time a player traded midseason had ever done so.

Small picture, short view: a tough pill to swallow; big picture, long view: trading Thornton was the best thing the Bruins could have done in the new millennium. Among other things, the salary cap space he freed up allowed for the long-term signing of future Cup champion captain Zdeno Chára.

"Yeah, well, don't be surprised if the Bruins win a Stanley Cup before the Sharks do," I said more than once. I'm a staunch believer in four essential factors in the sport of hockey, with its firehouse mentality requiring everyone fully on board for one another; they're what I call the Four Cs: coaching, chemistry, commitment, and character. As an observer, I was convinced the Bruins didn't have them all with Thornton, and his change of scenery would do everyone a world of good.

O'Connell lost his job with eleven games remaining in the regular season. Head coach Mike Sullivan lost his job during the summer. The men allegedly responsible for the horrible pre-lockout player personnel strategy that actually led to the dysfunctional roster and the shitty record, owner Jeremy Jacobs and his senior advisor, hockey legend Harry Sinden, lived to see another day.

The team had let its impending free agents walk before the autumn 2004 lockout, the extreme negotiating tool that cost the NHL and its fans an entire season. They had structured and timed contracts to expire before the work stoppage, an event everyone knew was coming three years in advance. The 2004–05 owners' lockout was utterly premeditated in an effort to secure a salary cap system of player revenue control for the league. But instead of a swath of free agents being available on the cheap, which the Bruins had hoped for coming out of the work stoppage, they were left with scraps. Via trade or free agency, Boston scrambled to fill the roster they had gutted by acquiring an aging Alexei Zhamnov, who missed most of the next season with a broken ankle, role player Dave Scatchard, limited power forward Brad Isbister, Brian Leetch, a great leader and Hall of Fame player on his last legs, and former Bruin Shawn McEachern, most of this in a desperate August 2005 signing binge.

By the way, before he was fired, O.C. also traded the Bruins other 1997 first-rounder, eighth overall pick, Sergei Samsonov, who actually won the Calder Trophy as Rookie of the Year in his and Thornton's first season. "Sammy" was an undersized left wing with great hands who had reached his ceiling and was moved to Edmonton for Marty Reasoner, Yan Stastny, and a second-round pick that turned out to be future Stanley Cup–winning core player Milan Lucic.

Not only did Boston go on to win the Cup before San Jose, who has yet to win one, but O'Connell eventually got his name on the silver chalice as well. In fact, he did it twice as an executive in the hockey department with the Los Angeles Kings. The Sharks, coy, almost mocking of the Bruins and O'Connell at the press conferences following the Thornton deal, have been consistent playoff failures. In the summer of 2014, they actually stripped Thornton of his team captaincy. In 2015, they failed to make the postseason. In 2016, they made their first-ever trip to the Stanley Cup Final and lost to Pittsburgh, and in 2017, they lost to Edmonton in the first round. By the way, Boston returned to the Final a second time in 2013 and lost to Chicago.

The only other Bruin at the Torino Olympics was P.J. Axelsson, also known as "Axie," for whom I had a keen interest. P.J., from his given name Per-Johan, always found time to talk hockey or life with me every time I approached him in the Bruins dressing room. We'd chat after practices. I'd work him into the informal rotation of post-practice or game sound bites I needed to get on camera on a regular basis for NESN. He was quirky, in that Swedish way: kind of flighty, yet aloof, like he was always in a hurry but had nowhere really to go. He wore those tight Euro suits with straight legs, baby-blue flood pants, and the like. He gave thoughtful answers, even after a loss, and generally smiled a lot. Plus, I had a fascination with Sweden — namely, the allure of Swedish women — and had narrowly missed several opportunities to get to Stockholm. I'd eventually make multiple trips to the beautiful country full of beautiful people, but it hadn't happened yet, and my curiosity and imagination about everything Swedish ran in overdrive.

In Torino, I made sure I checked in with Axie after every Team Sweden practice or in the mixed zone after his games. I was at all of them, and there was a secondary practical reason. NESN.com and Boston.com had me filing stories and a daily Olympic diary, which was the least I could do for them. The network had allowed me to go overseas for almost a month to work for someone else, an agreement I had arranged at the time of my hiring the previous fall. I had garnered the Olympic gig before I got the NESN job, and there was no way the latter was going to cancel out the former. Since management let me miss a handful of regular-season games, I happily agreed to provide some exclusive Olympic coverage for them in return.

Sweden started slowly and gradually got hot as the condensed tournament moved along. They were only the third seed in their group coming out of the preliminary round when they beat Switzerland 6–2 in the cross-overs to advance.

On February 24, Team Sweden whipped the Czech Republic in the semifinals to advance to the gold-medal game against their bitter rival and next-door neighbour Finland, who had shut out Russia 4–0. The championship game would take place on Sunday, February 26.

It was after the quarterfinal game that I had a momentous conversation with Axie, as he stood covered in sweat in the mixed zone. It wasn't a premeditated request; it just sort of hit me. But at that moment with Axie, given the significance of my job, the fact that it would likely be my only journey to the Games, and the fact we were both there from Boston, I cautiously and respectfully asked P.J. if, after the Games were over, I could have one of his sticks. I'm not an autograph or memorabilia collector by any stretch, I just thought that in this case an Olympic souvenir would be especially meaningful. Axie said, "Sure, absolutely." I wished him good luck and off he went.

On the final weekend of the Olympics, with only two games remaining in the tournament, I was now on a hockey vacation. My research wasn't required, with the intense scrutiny on, and preparation for, only four teams being handled by many other production people and the announcers themselves. I sat behind Doc and J.D. and watched the Czechs win the bronze medal over Russia on Saturday, and then simply looked forward to the gold-medal game. The eve of the final contest would be a festive night out in Torino.

During the Czech win, I ran into NHL referee Paul Devorski, one of the four men, two refs and two linesmen, officiating the final on Sunday.

"How you feeling about the game tomorrow, Devo?" I asked.

"Scared shitless," he said without changing his expression.

His blunt reply caught me off guard and I thought it was funny, but it really seemed like he wasn't kidding. He'd called big games before, but not in Europe, and not in a match between two bitter Scandinavian rivals and neighbours for the Olympic gold medal.

Devorski and fellow referee, Slovakian Milan Masik, would do an outstanding job. There would be no controversy.

The Palasport Olimpico rink was packed, raucous, and tense. I sat next to Doc and J.D.'s stats man, Ben Bouma, in the media zone of the stands for the first period. I could literally hear them calling the game *au naturel* from a couple seats away.

Finland scored first, with the lone goal of the first period. Kimmo Timonen from Selänne at 14:45 on the power play. In the second period, the Swedish Red Wings (there was an entire five-man unit from the Detroit roster on Team Sweden) took over. Henrik Zetterberg and Niklas Kronwall both scored on the power play to give Sweden the lead. It didn't last. With exactly five minutes left in the second, Ville Peltonen would tie things up on assists from the Jokinens, Jussi and Olli (no relation).

Twenty minutes (or more) left in the game to determine a winner, and it took all of ten seconds. On the opening face-off of the third period, Finnish centre Saku Koivu broke his stick, and in the time it took him to skate to the bench to get a new twig and get back into the play, the Swedes had taken advantage of what amounted to a brief four-on-three. Nicklas Lidstrom scored what would turn out to be the winning goal with a slap shot, at four-on-four even strength, on drop passes from Mats Sundin and Peter Forsberg.

That left nineteen minutes and fifty seconds of tension and frustration for Finnish fans. Their team had two power plays in the third and rang a shot off the goalpost, but they couldn't put one behind goalie Henrik Lundqvist. *Tre Kronor* were Olympic champions for the second time in history.

When the horn sounded, the Swedes went nuts. In an emotional ceremony, the two teams lined up at either end of the ice on rolled out carpets to get their medals. After the medals were presented, the Swedes went crazy again. Players skated all over, looking for family members and friends and Swedish fans and began tossing sticks and equipment into the stands. Some threw elbow pads, helmets, pretty much anything they could take off.

That's when I thought of Axie and spotted him almost at the exact same moment. He had tossed his gloves somewhere, and as he approached the far glass by the benches, he had his stick aloft, with one hand at the base, sort of in a ready-to-launch position. Just as he was starting the motion of sending that stick flying, he pulled it back, and then stepped off the ice and handed the stick to the Swedish equipment manager on the bench.

No way. No freaking way, I thought as I fell back into my seat.

The next couple of days were a whirlwind for everyone, especially Team Sweden, who partied overnight in Torino, then boarded a plane for a national celebration in Stockholm on Monday. Most of them then had to get back to North America to play for their respective NHL clubs no later than Wednesday, March 1. Many of them actually had a game on Tuesday night.

Axie and I had a Bruins game to play and broadcast on Wednesday in Carolina. He had an assist in the Bruins 4–3 loss, a blown lead. We chartered home to Boston after the game. I had kind of forgotten about the stick.

The next day's morning skate was completely optional, as is often the case before the second of back-to-back games. So I woke up, grabbed my coffee, and made it over to the TD Garden to watch the Atlanta Thrashers skate and pick up some notes on the game.

After lunch, I ran some errands, changed into a suit, and returned to the rink at about five o'clock. I was standing in the hall outside the NESN studio, across from the Boston dressing room, talking to Bruins defenceman Andrew Alberts. Suddenly, I spotted Axie approaching us from down the hall, carrying a hockey stick. My eyes lit up.

No way, I'm thinking again.

"Here's your stick, Simmer," Axie said, handing it to me.

I was speechless, my eyes misty. I fought my emotions and managed to thank him profusely. I grabbed a

Sharpie from one of our NESN techs, handed it to P.J., and watched him sign his gold-medal stick.

P.J. Axelsson played his last NHL game in the spring of 2009. He retired from pro hockey in 2013 after four seasons with the Frolunda team in Sweden. His left-handed "Made in Mexico" CCM Vector hangs in my office at home.

This was the call on Swedish TV of Tre Kronor *winning gold:*
"Get the puck out of the ZOOOONE! Jokinen has a great chance! Numminen, shot, YES! Lundqvist. Stand up!

Another shot! STRONG PLAY by Pebben [Axelsson]. YES!! OH YEAH!!!

Four, three . . . two . . . one, YES!

Ladies and gentlemen, Sweden is an Olympic champion in hockey. For the second time in history."

The closing seconds on NBC (1:05) found on YouTube: Torino Men's Hockey Gold

> "These sexual harassment charges
> . . . unmitigated lies."

**U.S. Senator Daniel Inouye,
October 1992**

DUMBASS *HAOLE*
BOY Part 1

When I left Hawaii for a new set of gigs on the mainland in January 1996, I cried like a baby. I couldn't help it. As my wife backed out of our driveway on Twelfth Avenue in Kaimuki, the lump in my throat grew to the size of a grapefruit. I tried to be a tough guy in front of her on the ride to the airport, but it was impossible. I teared up intermittently from the time I left the apartment until my flight was thirty minutes out of Honolulu.

I was *kama aina*. I was one with the *aina*. I knew, understood, and grasped the Aloha Spirit. The memories I had, the acquaintances and friendships I had made, and the life experiences gained thanks to residing on the most isolated island chain in the world were irreplaceable.

Among the many valuable lessons: I learned what it's like to be a minority. To feel what it was like to be disliked, hated in some cases, discriminated against, and ignored, simply because of the colour of my skin. In Hawaii, whites, or *haoles* ("how-lees"), are a distinct minority. They're disliked for a reason, dating back to 1893 when the United States imprisoned Queen Liliuokalani in her own palace and stole the islands.

I had moments of being discriminated against, and I get it. Tie in the historical equation and it's even easier to get. Unfortunately, non-locally raised white guys normally don't. It takes time, education, and growth to understand what makes the locals tick. Elsewhere, white guys are typically the ones doing the discriminating; they're rarely in a position to be treated as a minority. And they generally don't get a chance to learn that lesson.

Over time, I did come to feel welcome, partly because I was on TV. I would eventually become an anchor, first as a weatherman and then as a sports guy. This kind of visibility brought acceptance in this tough, athletic, patriarchal society. Had I been a stockbroker, or a government worker, or any other businessman from the mainland (USA), it would have been dramatically tougher to break through and embrace the true spiritual flavour and tradition of Hawaii.

When I arrived in Honolulu as a news reporter in November 1991, after a gig in Florida, I was anything but *kama aina* ("adopted local"). I was completely naïve; the prototypical dumb f'ing *haole*-boy from the mainland.

I first realized my lowly status thanks to a cameraman named Peter O'Callaghan, who worked at our station, the CBS affiliate KGMB-TV.

A week or two after arriving on Oahu, I bought the only car I could really afford, a 1971 Volkswagen Bug, for $600. It didn't have a paint job; it was essentially the colour of primer, with multicoloured blotches and rust spots, and its front hood (which is the storage compartment on a Beetle) had to be tied down with a shoelace to keep it from flying up and off. The floor in front of the passenger seat had actually rusted through in spots, and you could see the road passing beneath the car. It was beach buggy 101.

Despite all of the car's weaknesses, the engine was in tremendous condition. It hummed. Had I been in an accident, it likely would have happened while I was moving along rather nicely. Unfortunately, the car itself would have disintegrated, taking me along with it.

The cost to insure one's car in Hawaii has always been ridiculously high, just one example of many filed under "price of paradise." Had I used a major insurance company such as State Farm or Allstate, I would have paid twice the value of my car each year on insurance. Through a newsroom tip, via the military, I learned about GEICO, which literally stood for Government Employees Insurance Company, but you didn't have to be a government employee to buy a policy. I had never heard of it and their rates were secretly low. Almost thirty years later, they're known only by the acronym and have become a national marketing behemoth.

Lopaka and Lopaka.

I loved my Bug. I could easily change my own oil — it was like changing the oil on a lawn mower — and I figured if the engine ever fell out, I could run with my feet through the floor and propel it like I was Fred Flintstone.

O'Callaghan, the rambunctious Irish cameraman, convinced me I should have a name for my car, following an alleged Hawaiian tradition. He also convinced me I should name it Lopaka, or "little smoke."

"That's *Lo*, as in 'little,' in Hawaiian," he said, "and *paka*, as in *pakalolo* [Hawaiian for 'marijuana']. See, little smoke," he finished.

"Cool," I replied. "Little Smoke, that's perfect."

This loud and playful conversation took place across the crowded KGMB newsroom.

A few days later, after making the rounds, bragging about my new car Lopaka, I'd come to learn that *Lopaka* in Hawaiian actually meant Robert.

Not only was there no tradition of car naming, I had just named the car after myself.

This little practical joke was obviously harmless, but not long after, when I crossed paths with the most powerful politician in the archipelago, the fact that I was a dumbass *haole* boy had much more serious implications.

The Hawaii Democrats literally owned the state, a political machine so effectively entrenched it would be difficult to imagine duplication. Democrats made up the entire congressional delegation and the party proportions in the state legislature would best be described as a joke. The Republicans generally held two or three senate seats out of two dozen each session, and maybe 10 percent or less of the state house. On occasion, you could throw in a representative from the Green or Libertarian Party.

At the national level, there was periodic upheaval in Washington, D.C., as the balance of power frequently, and sometimes dramatically, shifted between the Democrats and Republicans in Congress and in the Senate, like in 1994 when the GOP took over. But the proportion of Democrats to Republicans in Hawaii rarely saw change. The Democratic domination spanned four decades.

Among that contingent sat the king — the leader, the demigod, the living embodiment of the Hawaii Democrats in national politics — United States Senator Daniel Inouye ("In-oh-way"). First voted into a D.C. office as a congressman when Hawaii became a state in 1959, he was first elected to the Senate in 1962. Eventually, six years, by six years, by six years, by six years, by six years, by six years, by six years, by six years, by six years, by six years, he was re-elected, eventually becoming the second-longest tenured U.S. senator in history.

It's no wonder he made a name for himself. He sat in the national limelight during the Senate hearings on Watergate and the Nixon fiasco, and he went on to chair important committees, like the Senate Armed Services.

At home and around the world, Inouye was a well-respected hero. He grew up the son of Japanese immigrants in the 1920s and 1930s in Honolulu, and while fighting for his family's adopted country in World War II, he battled valiantly, lost an arm, earned the Bronze Star, the Purple Heart, and later the Medal of Honor for his heroism in fighting the Germans in Italy. He came home, went into politics, and had remained there ever since.

"Relatively automatic" would best describe Inouye's re-election chances for November 1992; obviously not an easy hill to climb if you happened to be Inouye's election opponent.

Undaunted by Inouye's credentials, Rick Reed, Republican state senator representing Maui, attempted to climb that hill. Originally a mainland *haole*, and a former Washington State University defensive back, Reed wore his competitiveness on his sleeve. Apparently, he was fearless and would use whatever means necessary to win.

Tuesday, October 13, 1992.
I had worked at KGMB for just eleven months when

the biggest scandal ever to rock Hawaii politics was dropped in my lap. I went from covering a story on a controversial permit for a putt-putt golf course in the morning to covering the biggest political story since statehood.

I was researching mini-golf legalities when our receptionist, Anita, walked up behind me.

"Rob, there's someone here to see you," she said.

"Who?"

"Some girl. Says it's real important," she answered. "Needs to see you right now."

"Never a problem," I said, standing up, undaunted by the pregnancy innuendos hurled my way by my esteemed colleagues in the newsroom.

I made my way to the reception area to meet this mystery girl. A thin, almost gaunt, plain-looking woman in her midtwenties nervously introduced herself. Her name was Umeko Walker and she held something in her hands that she insisted I had to see and hear. I led her into a small conference room.

"No one has sent me. I'm doing this on my own," she was quick to say.

(Oddly enough, a few months later in this same conference room, our assignment editor, Brenda, had me sit and listen to another random story, this time from an Australian couple who told me about conditions at a religious commune they had lived at in Waco, Texas. They were heading back home "down under" and stopped in Honolulu to tell their story because they knew of Hawaii residents who lived at the complex in Waco. It was the Branch Davidian compound of David Koresh. We didn't feel we should cover the story, based mostly on jurisdiction and cost. In 1993, a late-February raid by the U.S. Government led to ten deaths, including four federal agents, and eventually to the siege and fire that killed Koresh and seventy-five of his cohabitants.)

With that, Walker handed me a couple of cassette tapes and began to describe them. The tapes held secretly recorded conversations between Walker and Dan Inouye's longtime barber, Lenore Kwock. On tape, Walker interviews Kwock as Kwock describes being sexually molested by the senator. Walker also handed me a transcript of the entire recording.

My head spun with excitement, then doubt, then mistrust.

Walker denied that she was working for Reed, and insisted on leaving rather quickly, to pass out copies of the tape to the rest of the media. She said she had another tape for me and agreed to bring it, and sit down for an interview the next day. At this point, it was three o'clock. We were approaching deadline and a decision had to be made.

Bob Jones, the most veteran reporter, managing editor, and interim news director, picked a great time to be out of town and off the islands. That left it up to Jade Moon, former model turned TV reporter and anchor, to make the biggest decision of our careers.

The tape recordings sounded legitimate. We placed calls to the Reed campaign, the Inouye campaign, and to Kwock's salon. Both of us leaned towards going with the story, and after just a few minutes of thought, we did. It led the six o'clock news.

I sat next to Jade on the set and described the situation and played excerpts from the tape. The KGMB audience listened to Lenore Kwock describe being "molested" by Senator Inouye.

I could feel my adrenaline pumping and could see that Jade's was also. We had made a huge decision. One that could be career-threatening, if not life-threatening, I really didn't know.

We promised more on our late newscast, and I hopped off the set almost breathless. It was the start of a sometimes-hellish four weeks.

The phone calls came pouring in. The Inouye Campaign was in disbelief. Stunned viewers jammed the lines. I couldn't help but think that somewhere, Rick Reed was laughing deviously.

After consulting the station's attorney and having talked to the Inouye camp, our station general manager Dick Grimm, who was every bit his name, pulled the story from the ten o'clock news. I was a little bit pissed off but not surprised. Jade took the decision calmly. It just meant a lot of digging had to be done over the next twenty-four hours.

The next day, Wednesday, I recorded the only interview ever done with the mysterious Umeko Walker.

"This is something I did completely on my own," she reaffirmed. "My own trip, nobody gave me instructions and told me what to do. I just, this is something I felt I had to do. I just feel like it's an important enough issue, that other women should be forewarned, they should know about Dan Inouye's history and what he's done. I feel a deep responsibility to other women, so this doesn't happen again."

By Thursday, her deep responsibility apparently came to an end. Walker fell off the face of the earth. The newspapers and other media outlets tried in vain to find her. We had the only picture, audio, and interview with the "bringer of bad tidings."

Her disappearance seemed awfully convenient for Rick Reed, who denied having anything to do with the revelation of the tapes. He claimed the taped conversation was a complete surprise to him as well, that Walker had dropped a copy off at his headquarters on Tuesday.

However, Reed's denials became more difficult to swallow as time went by. As it turned out, Walker had allegedly worked for the Reed campaign during the previous summer but had quit over an unknown disagreement. Also, both Walker and Reed had apparent ties to Reed's Hare Krishna mentor on Maui.

To get the tapes exposed to the public with the least amount of initial scrutiny, I was the perfect conduit — a novice Hawaii reporter, not well-versed in the political histories of the parties involved. I had interviewed Reed on a few occasions and enjoyed pleasant conversations with him. He knew I was inexperienced in the Hawaii political scene. He also knew the election was in less than a month.

In order to catch Reed in what appeared each day to be more and more like an intricate scheme, we attempted a little trickery of our own. Three days after the story broke, on Friday, I arranged to meet Reed at a nearby park on the south shore, about three blocks from the TV station. I told him it was to update him on the situation and to get his feelings on the matter, one-on-one.

I drove there alone in Lopaka, wearing a hidden wireless microphone. We duct taped the microphone's transmitting unit to the inside of my thigh, inside my pants. A wire ran up my shirt to a small microphone, which was taped to my left shoulder, facing out to the left. When I arrived at Ala Moana Beach Park, I hopped out of Lopaka and sat on the two-foot-high concrete wall that ran along the edge of the roadway. Small waves rolled in and children played on the beach behind me. Our cameraman, Sisto Domingo, sat in his car, parallel parked about fifty yards to my right. His camera sat on his lap, with the attached microphone receiver. When Reed passed in his car, we both activated the audio.

I sat with a queasy stomach. I pictured getting caught. If he admitted something first, and then saw the microphone, it wouldn't matter. I could say, "Ha, gotcha," and walk away. This was legal in Hawaii. But if he caught me first, without having said anything, I'd feel like a diabolical heel not being able to capture the proof I sought. I kind of felt like one anyway.

Luckily, the candidate parked to my left and sat on my left. I wouldn't have to switch "seats" as he was talking directly into my left shoulder.

"How are you holdin' up?" I asked.

"Pretty good," he answered. "It's really been a bit crazy. I feel bad for Lenore — she's taking a beating."

"Today at noon, she meets the press," I told him. "At her salon, we'll get right into it."

"Well, it's bad news, but news people should know about," Reed responded. He then went on to describe how he would help bring forth the message about sexual assault and its evils. I didn't know it, but at this point, my mic transmission started to fade out.

"C'mon man, what's the deal with Umeko? You guys

had nothing to do with this?" I probed, nervous with anticipation.

Reed would make a statement similar to those he had made publicly earlier in the week.

"I heard several rumours in the past. I had never heard [Kwock's] name or the specifics until Tuesday of this past week. And when I listened to this tape when we got it about noon, I was shaken by it and convinced by it."

Despite being an acquaintance, Reed wasn't about to reveal any potential secrets to me and take any chance of blowing his campaign, off the record or not.

At the end of the conversation came a very tense moment. As Reed said farewell to me, he put his hand on the back of my shoulder as he talked. His hand missed the microphone by about an inch. Panic shot through me.

"Okay, well, I'll talk to you later," I said while standing up and extending my hand. He took his hand off my shoulder and shook mine.

"Good luck," I added.

"You, too, see ya later," he said. "Let me know how it goes with Lenore," he added as he walked off.

"I'm sure you'll hear about it," I responded.

Whew. I had reacted quickly, but the last ten seconds had seemed like ten minutes. The secret meeting had failed. Reed's involvement in the Walker tape recording would remain purely speculative.

As Reed had mentioned, at this point, the biggest victim in the alleged scandal, was hairdresser Lenore Kwock. It was obvious that she had no idea she was revealing the Inouye information on tape. During the disclosures, the sound was a bit muffled, as Walker kept the microphone hidden, and ambient "elevator" music from the salon could be heard in the background.

"I had no idea that Umeko Walker was recording all of this secretly without my knowledge," she told the large group of reporters at her salon on Friday. "Her intention was devious. I did not consent to this. I thought I was helping a young lady."

In 1975, Kwock worked at a hair salon in the Ilikai Hotel in Waikiki. Kwock told the story of how her boss asked her to pick up a jumpsuit from the senator's apartment.

"He grabbed me right as I came through the door and began making his advances on me. So it was him who removed my clothing and proceeded on, by then in my mind I realized, this is going to happen."

Kwock said the two of them had sex, but that it wasn't rape, possibly just coercion or intimidation. She said she decided to continue to cut the senator's hair after the first incident.

"For me, I forgive him, and I actually bless him and wish him well, which is why I still took him [as a customer]. I realize this man has a problem, and I feel sorry for him."

Months after the first encounter, Kwock said she became angry after another incident.

"As I was washing his hair, he just reached up my dress, right up to my crotch, and it was shocking to me and humiliating, and degrading and I panicked. I didn't know what to do, but from that moment on I was so afraid of this man," she concluded.

She was afraid to confront him *and* to cut his hair. On the taped interview, Kwock explained her fears of revealing the incidents.

"Dan," she said, "everyone knows about his reputation. He'll still be in office, but he'll come and get you. He has all the connections to do it."

Gee, just what I wanted to hear.

For fifteen years, Kwock had kept the issue and the alleged incidents a secret, but at some point, she slipped up. She must have told the story to a customer, who eventually leaked the information to Walker, or to whoever sent Walker. Then Walker, under the guise of a crusader for women's rights, got Kwock to talk and secretly tape recorded it.

Of course, by Friday, Reed was using the tape recordings of Kwock in his thirty- and sixty-second campaign commercials entitled "Rape and Daniel Inouye."

NARRATOR: "Has Daniel Inouye misused his position as our U.S. senator to exploit women? Here's what his barber of twenty years says Inouye did to her."

KWOCK (FROM TAPE): "I just felt a lot of force and intimidation and that kind of feeling, and everything just happened so quickly I didn't know what to do."

WALKER (FROM TAPE): "Did he say anything?"

KWOCK (FROM TAPE): "No! I came through the door, I remember . . . I remember just stepping in and remember him grabbing me and it was just so . . . whoa! Everything was so fast."

Meanwhile, my role in the scandal had reached one of its many points of frustration. Our GM, Dick Grimm, wouldn't let us run various elements of the story throughout the week, including, at one point, the exclusive Umeko Walker interview. He called me upstairs to his office to debate the validity of the story. Not the validity of the source, or of the tape recordings, or of the legal ramifications, but the validity of Kwock's description of rape.

I couldn't believe it. Dozens of issues swirled around this story, and my general manager was trying to decide if Inouye sticking his hand up a woman's skirt was sexual assault. To be quite honest, I didn't know. I did know our boss was concerned about the station potentially taking a bath from a major lawsuit or two, alienating the most powerful man in Hawaii politics, and pissing off all of his constituents, and I can only imagine the heat he was taking from politically active TV advertisers. I viewed it as a reporter; he viewed it as a businessman.

Grimm and I argued, and at one point he told me I couldn't run the story about Walker discussing women's rights and sexual assault, and I left.

Fortunately by the end of the week, and after Kwock's Friday press conference, the rest of the local TV stations had cautiously jumped on the bandwagon. It then became a full-blown circus, at least by Hawaii standards.

That's another of the many nice things about reporting news on the most isolated islands in the world: even a big, obnoxious story never really gets that big and obnoxious. Had this been a mainland man of comparable stature with comparable allegations — holy cow!

The "circus" however, did take the pressure off our GM, and it did allow me the chance to run the entire Walker interview late Friday, our second exclusive scoop of the week.

Meanwhile, the Democratic Party and its most prominent figure, silent to this point, were taking a beating.

In her interview, Kwock said, "The Democratic Party, the way they talk, it's, yeah, we are aware of the dark side of him and we know a lot of people have mistresses, and then they try to shove it under the rug because they have to protect his image."

As one might imagine, at this point I ranked just below Ronald Reagan on the Democrats' popularity list and was known as the *haole* jackass "who started this mess with the senator." My sudden notoriety made it very difficult for me to follow additional leads in the unfolding story. One of our more veteran island reporters, Jerry Drelling, although often assigned to the police beat, was more than anxious to pick up a big portion of the load. It was the story of the decade. He'd follow Inouye around while I chased down others.

We talked to Inouye, Reed, Kwock, their family members, the party chairman from each side, the minor party candidates, and men and women on the street. We were taking call-in polls on who in the scandal was the biggest "scumbag." I garnered a couple votes.

It was stressful, it was fun, and it was all within the scandal's first four days.

"This is ridiculous.
You're in deep trouble."

My boss to me, on the news set,
October 1992

DUMBASS *HAOLE* BOY Part 2

We broke the harassment allegations on Tuesday. By Friday, Senator Daniel Inouye was speaking out.

"For a long time, we felt that this was just a mainland kind of campaigning," the senator announced. "But now we find it's here; resorting to sleazy slime, guilt by innuendo, guilt by association. Well, I'm not going to take this sitting down."

As horrendous as the scandal was becoming, the mudslinging did provide Inouye an easy escape from a potentially undesirable obligation. He used the sleaze as an excuse to dismiss any hope for a debate. Opponent Rick

Reed would not have the opportunity to confront Inouye on his senatorial voting record.

"After this demonstration of slime and sleaze, after all the demonstrations [Reed] had in the night-time flyers, sleazy ad on the Keating Five . . . I can tell you the debate is a moot question," the senator concluded.

The Keating Five was in reference to an investigation of a savings-and-loan financial scandal involving five U.S. senators in the 1980s. Inouye wasn't one of the five.

Meanwhile, our interim news director and anchor, Bob Jones, continued his off-island business, and none of the other "hierarchy" within our newsroom knew which stories to run and which angles to kill.

By Friday evening, I had received a number of calls from political correspondent Rita Braver from CBS News, anxious to get updates as often as possible. CBS showed portions of our newscast on *its* newscast, mentioning that we had broken the story. Braver apologized for the fact that those clips didn't include shots of me on the set. I didn't care. Contrary to conventional thinking for a reporter looking for exposure, I was content with as much anonymity as possible at this point. I was more concerned with my well-being in the Islands, as I wasn't planning on leaving any time soon.

In the end, I think CBS eventually did about a story and a half on Inouye, mostly tied into other scandals around the country during "Election '92." There was never a network-level Inouye story unto itself.

I took Saturday off; the story, of course, did not. My colleague Jerry Drelling reported the fact that Reed had pulled his "rape" campaign commercials off the air. That decision came after Lenore Kwock pleaded with him to do so. The two finally agreed that Kwock had suffered enough humiliation on the airwaves as a result of her revelation, and that good taste suggested a change in strategy. Of course, Reed probably already felt pretty confident he had successfully established an anti-Inouye campaign platform.

Meanwhile, the Inouye camp's attempt to simply sweep the allegations under the rug was a lesson in futility. Even in the senator's Democratic fiefdom, this scandal was tough to shove aside. His best option was the "family values" strategy, a popular concept during this time period. Mainland politicians who were drunks, or pill poppers, or adulterers would grab the wife and kids and stand in front of a church and say, "I'm good." It was like a rhetorical get-out-of-jail-free card. It came from the "image is everything" cache, also known as the "let's just see how gullible my constituents are" strategy. More often than not, gullible and ignorant went hand in hand.

Enter Mrs. Inouye.

On Sunday, I was back at work and did something I had never done before as a reporter or as a "civilian." I attended a fashion show. Mr. and Mrs. Inouye were there as a team. Both spoke about the scandalous allegations to a crowd mostly made up of hundreds of women. The female constituents appeared to dismiss the allegations as nonsense as they applauded and cheered approvingly when the two discussed their decades of marital bliss. Following the speeches, the Inouyes briefly met the media.

"I support Dan, I love Dan, I don't believe any of this," Maggie Inouye stated. (After fifty-seven years of marriage,

Interviewing a historian outside of Iolani Palace on the 100th anniversary of the U.S. overthrowing the Queen. The windows were shrouded in black curtains.

Maggie passed away in 2006. The senator married his second wife, Irene, a prominent California patron of the arts and philanthropic socialite, in 2008.)

I actually felt bad for Mrs. Inouye, yet another victim in this swirling mess. Whether the allegations were true or not, she was confronted with an ugly situation.

I was conflicted. This was the only time I really felt pangs of guilt for my role in the scoop. At the same time, why should I feel guilty? I was simply the original public messenger, second only to the mysterious Umeko Walker.

To calm my mind, I tried to stress and reiterate what Sophocles once said, as did Shakespeare in *Henry IV*: don't kill the messenger.

I forced myself to brush off the emotions. Unfortunately, the senator didn't make the adjustment that easily. He glared at me as I asked him and his wife a question.

Later that day, I interviewed a political analyst on the impact of the scandal on the election campaign, and then I spoke to a women's rights attorney about her take on things. All of these angles made up a pretty solid Sunday newscast.

I took a day off from Inouye on Monday. Instead, I did a story about the minor party candidates running for the senate seat. From my perspective as a voter, the Green and Libertarian Party candidates were looking better and better every day. They weren't professional politicians and they weren't bought. They made sense, they talked about the issues that really mattered, and they made me temporarily forget about being dragged through the slop by those two other dudes.

Ultimately, this election, like any other, was about power and money, money and power. And of course, it was about one guy winning the right to get paid decent money to be a "public servant" and hang out in D.C. as a VIP.

Whether in Alabama, Florida, or Hawaii — all places I have worked in TV news — I never quite figured out the public-servant deal, especially when it came to U.S. senators. People would treat these guys like royalty, ready to kiss their rings. I'd be thinking, *Hey, dipshits, this guy is supposed to be serving you, not giving himself a raise every few years, flying around on junkets on your dime, living in the lap of luxury, and serving special interest groups (and their money) before anything else.* But, you know, that's pretty much how it works.

The following Tuesday, a week after the original story

broke, our very supportive and delightful assignment editor, Brenda Salgado, came up with the idea of a little scandal recap starring yours truly. I loved this idea, since I already had a good idea on how to put it together, and besides, that Tuesday brought little fresh information to report. It would be our little one-week anniversary scandal special.

The recap would involve sound bites from every person involved and fancy preproduced graphics to help lay out the events chronologically.

Had this been 2017, the graphics guy would have been done putting together what I wanted in about fifteen minutes and would have emailed it to the cameraman/editor or handed it to him on a jump drive. Or the cameraman/editor would have been able to do the simple graphic effects themself on their computer editing system. Television shows are put together the same way. Interview material (sound bites), video ("cover"), stand-ups (reporter-on-camera shots), and audio track (reporter voice) are all loaded off a disc or video card onto a computer. Like linking little train cars together electronically, the editor follows the reporter's written script and puts the video and audio pieces end-to-end so they all mesh together delightfully. Each piece can be trimmed, tightened, and fit snugly with a quick click of the mouse.

In 1992, in the sixty-third largest TV market in the country, we were still doing what is called linear editing, and building graphics took time, effort, and a written request. The main news control room was used to build any special effects in advance of the live show.

Despite the fact that I had finished writing the piece by noon and had isolated the sound bites I wanted, I had to wait until at least three o'clock to get my preproduction started. That's when the director and the other technical staff members came to work in the control room to prepare for the show.

The three o'clock start was a built-in liability. Often, preproduction requests would pile up and reporters would have to wait until late in the afternoon to get their finished product. Again, the intricate graphics and special effects for the story could not be done in the normal editing booth. The cameraman/editor didn't have the technology.

For the Inouye recap, I had a number of funky on-screen moves. Umeko Walker, Rick Reed, Daniel Inouye, and Lenore Kwock would all appear together on the screen in four individual little boxes. As my voice began to describe each individual, their box and picture would come forward and fill the screen completely. After their sound bite ended or I finished discussing each person, their little box would sink back into the set of four, and then the next person's image would move forward.

Once the preproduction was finished in the control room, these graphic effects still had to be edited into the final story by the photographer/editor in one of four edit bays (tiny rooms). Linear editing, or editing tape machine–to–tape machine, took time. The other reporters and I actually did quite a bit of it ourselves. The on-air sports guys at the station did all of their own edits.

A master tape, where the story would end up, would be inserted into the machine on the right. Here, we would assemble the story. In and out of the tape machine on the left, we would alternate between the tape with the reporter's scripted voice track on it and the field tapes with the sound bites and video on them. The editor would set an edit in-point on both machines by pushing two buttons simultaneously. The tapes would rewind three or four seconds, then roll forward to that dub in-point and continue. As they kept rolling, the master tape would record what was on the field tape. It would record until you hit a button to stop them. Then he'd cue up the master tape to the end point of that first cut, put a new tape in the left machine, pick a starting spot for the next piece, cue it, and lay it on the master tape using the same recording method. This would go on until the entire combination of audio, bites, and video was laid down on the master. In the case of my story, the editor would then do a "video only" overlay, and roll the graphics over the top of the existing edited material in the appropriate positions. (And to think fifteen years before this, they were still building news stories by editing film!)

A couple big problems arose for my Inouye recap. First, my editor, Terry Hunter, was late getting back from shooting another story, and it wasn't until he arrived that he actually found out he was editing mine. Secondly, the preproduction took longer than expected and was running late. Therefore, *I'd* be late.

For the first time in the KGMB portion of my career, I'd miss my assigned slot in a show. I sat on the set with co-anchors Jones and Moon, ready to introduce the top story of the six o'clock news with a little question-and-answer session.

With the top story not ready, the producer, who stacked the show's content, panicked in the control room. He scrambled to rearrange items, making the necessary adjustments in the show order, while the anchors shuffled their scripts on the set, trying to figure out where to go next.

Producers talk to anchors via earpieces they're wearing, called IFBs (interruptible feedback), while the producer can obviously hear what the anchors are saying through their microphones.

The news is live television, making it imperative that reporters and editors always make their deadline. Missing a slot can screw up an entire show and make the anchors look like dorks. That's the riskiest thing about anchoring news, sports, or weather. Regardless of who makes the mistake, when or where, the anchor is the one sitting in front of thousands (or millions) of people, potentially looking like the idiot.

Welcome to my personal hell. In this case, we were ultra-late. Not only did we miss the top-story slot, we missed the entire first block of news. Then, we missed the entire second block.

At each of the breaks, I got queasier. Bob Jones would swear, shake his head, and talk shit about my performance with the producer. Moon would just give me a "tsk" and look at me painfully. I didn't need the humiliation. I was already so pissed off at myself I couldn't stand it. While Jones moaned during the breaks, I'd lean back and yell down the hallway, "How we doin'? Done yet?" It may have been the longest fifteen minutes of my life.

My live introduction and three-minute recap came at the top of the third block. This is normally where a story about a one-legged surfer or a pineapple-picking competition airs, just before we tease what's coming up in sports.

The story was everything I had dreamed of all day long. It was beautiful, it was thorough, and the preproduction worked perfectly. All of this meant absolutely nothing, since it was twelve minutes late.

When it finally ran, no one on the set paid attention to the story; everyone remained rattled. I hopped off the set when I was done and quickly left the building, embarrassed and fuming.

The added gnarliness to this whole thing was my relationship with Jones. When he had returned to the anchor chair and to running the newsroom the previous day, it came as no surprise when he indicated I was to be taken off the Inouye story. Jones was still putting me through his personal wringer for the eleventh straight month, for whatever reason, and in the limelight was the last place he wanted me.

His was a strange resentment I've never completely been able to figure out.

Maybe due to the "big fish, small pond" phenomenon, local anchors' egos are gargantuan, even compared to most widely known national TV figures I've worked around, which makes Will Ferrell's portrayal of Ron Burgundy in *Anchorman* all the more entertaining. Of course the movie was exaggerated, but much of the nonsense and self-centeredness rings true.

Reporters would mispronounce Hawaiian words, show up late, miss deadlines, and they'd never hear a word of criticism. I'd misspell a word in a script and I'd be threatened with a pink slip. My long-term strategy to deal with this weirdness was to hang low and stay as inconspicuous as possible. The Inouye fallout made that difficult. The recap delay screw-up made it almost impossible. Jones had a legitimate gripe.

The next day, I arrived to find the predictable email from Jones. I was incompetent, he was tired of the mistakes, and I needed to be fired. This I couldn't ignore. It was ridiculous. It was my first error of any kind in months and the only major screw-up of my tenure. In my mind at the time, I had no excuse for messing up (although I actually had a couple) and I took responsibility, but the harassment had to stop. I replied to Jones's threatening email with my own rebuttal, sent it to him and to GM Grimm, and then printed it out and put it on the newsroom bulletin board. It basically said, "Stop the bullshit and let me do my job." It was the best note I've ever written.

Wednesday turned out to be easy, probably thanks to assignment editor Salgado looking out for me. I interviewed another woman from a women's rights group, then conducted an interview on an unrelated topic, and finished up early. Thursday and Friday would be uneventful in terms of new developments and just as mellow, which was exactly what I needed.

Although not much of an actor, I auditioned for a play at a local theatre each night that week, which served as the perfect distraction from Bob Jones, Senator Inouye, and associates. Eventually, through the media/theatre grapevine, I landed speaking parts and a role as an extra in a few network television programs that were shot in Hawaii. Just like news reporters and anchors before me who managed to sneak onto *Hawaii Five-O* in the 1970s (such as Bob Jones himself) or *Magnum, P.I.* in the 1980s, I snagged a couple of gigs on shows that would never go on to be as successful. One might draw a correlation between the failure of those programs and the level of talent they were using to round out the productions.

When they weren't shooting on location, these productions shot the remainder of their material in a studio about six blocks from my apartment, over a hill behind Diamond Head where the Kaimuki neighbourhood ended and the Kahala area began.

I earned my coveted Screen Actors Guild union card for appearing on *Raven*, starring Lee Majors (the six-million-dollar man) and some dude named Jeffrey Meek, who played a special forces, martial-arts specialist. Local comedian Andy Bumatai played a character named "The Big Kahuna." In one episode, I played the host of *America's Most Dangerous*, a show on which Majors's character is mistaken for a serial killer. I never was on set with any of these people.

Three years later I played a local TV sportscaster — quite a stretch, since at the time I was a local TV sportscaster — in a segment shot right on our news set. In the role, I introduced a story about a sumo wrestler who had been murdered; the show was *One West Waikiki*, starring Cheryl Ladd. Unfortunately, I didn't get to actually work with her either.

In between, I was an extra on another show that never made it, *The Byrds of Paradise*, starring Timothy Busfield (the red-headed guy from *Thirtysomething* who also played reporter Danny Concannon on *The West Wing*). What jumped out of this production was the emergence of the people playing his two older kids. Seth Green played the eldest son and Jennifer Love Hewitt played his character's sister. Green, among other things, went on to play the son of Dr. Evil in the Mike Myers's Austin Powers movies. I did actually get to hang around these people on set and I remember thinking about Jennifer, *this young lady is gonna be beautiful when she gets older.* Yeah, I know, it didn't take a genius.

Lie detector tests became the next angle on the scandal. Our police reporter, Jerry Drelling, handled that part of the story because it was retired Honolulu Police polygrapher, Mike Orion, who would be administering the tests and analyzing the results. Lenore Kwock took the test and passed with flying colours, reaffirming everyone's gut feeling that Kwock was not a liar. Senator Inouye danced around the issue for a few days and then refused to take a polygraph.

Drelling asked the senator if he had any reason to doubt the expertise of Orion.

"I don't know Mr. Orion, I've never met him," the senator said. "I'm not aware of his credentials . . . I suppose he's a credible person. But I saw part of his statement when he said it's very reliable and he as a polygraph — whatever title you have — should know better than that. Can we go to something else?" Good idea, Senator.

Despite the lie detector refusal and the growing debate over the senator's past, his lead in the polls actually grew a little bit with just over seven days to the election. Public sentiment seemed to be against Reed for his suspected role in bringing the scandal forward, more so than against the senator, even if many believed Inouye guilty. Part of this was simply "f'ing *haole* boy" versus local. Reed came across as a disingenuous *haole* originally from the mainland, while Inouye was as local-Japanese as local-Japanese could get.

One important resource who wasn't available during this entire mess was the senator's right-hand man and spokesman in Washington, D.C., Nestor Garcia. Nestor had worked as a news reporter in Honolulu for a while but decided on politics instead. He knew our entire news staff rather well, was close friends with a few of my cohorts, but offered little or no help during these proceedings. His role during the campaign was hands off, an interesting dynamic. The Washington staff was kept apart from the Hawaii election staff, at least publicly, and this seemed to serve the senator well. Plus it meant the full-time staff could "play dumb" once they arrived back in D.C. and could avoid having to answer any questions.

While Garcia kept his distance in the final weeks leading up to the election in Hawaii, the role of public relations consultant, or media assistant, on the ground fell to hired hand Marie Reyko. Reyko was apparently instructed to make my job as difficult as possible, and she followed instructions perfectly. "Uncooperative and nasty" was my term for her performance during those couple of weeks. (Less than a year later, I ran into her at a concert and she admitted to being horrible, but insisted she was only doing her job. I couldn't blame her. The most powerful public figure in Hawaii was footing the bill.)

Despite the Inouye camp's obvious dislike for me and their lack of cooperation, our news management decided to put me back on the beat right before the election. The perfect capper came when Jones insisted that I handle the live shots and the interviews from Inouye's campaign headquarters during election night. More of an intentional manoeuvre, I reckon, rather than an obvious error in judgement.

The evening unfolded as expected. Inouye won by a landslide, narrower than most of his victories, but still by almost a two-to-one margin.

The Democratic machine had chewed up the scandal and spit it out.

As the senator and his cronies celebrated with the crowd, I and the other TV reporters, who had assembled at various positions around the ballroom, set up for our final live shots. After reporting the results and the reaction, our last task would be to interview the victor.

Fat chance.

Inouye talked to Channel 2 for a few minutes, live. Then he briefly chatted with the Channel 4 reporter. When he finished, I tried to distract him, our on-site producer tried to grab him, as did one of his campaign assistants. Our camera was set up right inside the door to the building. The senator turned away from us, slid in between a couple of his very large Samoan body guards, and passed us like we had the bubonic plague. He didn't even shoot us a look, just smirked as he passed by. The most powerful politician in Hawaii, and the prize interview of the night, walked right out the door.

Momentarily I was upset, at him, at Jones, at the whole damn scene. Then I realized it was over. I sighed. A weight had been lifted.

No more mudslinging, no more runarounds, no more lies.

No more politics.

———————

Rick Reed, living back in the state of Washington, is an executive at a marketing firm.

In December 2012, two years after winning his ninth term in 2010, Senator Inouye died at the age of eighty-eight. His body lay in state in the U.S. Capitol Rotunda, only the thirty-first person, and the first Asian-American, to receive such an honour.

Not long after the 1992 election, nine other women alleged harassment against Inouye, via a female state legislator, but none would participate in a full inquiry. In 2014, two years after his death, Inouye was accused of sexually harassing fellow senator Kirsten Gillibrand.

COLLEGE KLEPTO

That's it, time to come clean. It was me, the radio play-by-play guy, the voice of Chippewa Baseball, who stole the 325-foot marker. My overwhelming sentimentality for the game got the best of me. More to the point, so did eight beers and a couple shots of tequila.

One day, I was sitting in the press box calling the action of Central Michigan University baseball, making reference to the 325-foot stretch down the right and left field lines, 375 feet or whatever it was to the power alleys, and 400 feet to straightaway centerfield. The next day, early in the first inning I went with, "It's 325 down the lines here at Alumni Field . . . hey, wait, the marker in left field appears to be missing. That's odd."

Despite being hungover and a lousy actor, I got away with it. I was somewhat well respected in student media circles and a pretty decent play-by-play guy. No one in the press box that day would suspect me of stealing the sign the night before. My secret was safe, until now.

What happened in the dark of night between those two baseball broadcasts was a secret I had planned to take to my grave. Then my ten-year-old son asked me one day, "Hey, Dad, what's that big metal sign in your closet mean?"

"Well, son, I was hammered one night, didn't get laid, so I decided while I was walking home in the middle of the night to rip it off the outfield wall at my college ball-park." This is the explanation *I didn't go with*. I think I said it was a gift. Realizing I was just compounding the evil, I've decided to tell the real story, which begs the question, can I still be charged or punished?

Central Michigan University was an all-around delightful experience. The education was decent, not at the level of the University of Michigan or one of the bratty, small private schools around the state, but decent enough. We had a very solid regional broadcasting program. Just as important, it was a flourishing party school in those days, sixteenth on the *Playboy* national list of party schools, with horny and hot suburban and small-town coeds ready to experiment. Utopia, some would call it; the party atmosphere was the main reason I extended my attendance to five years.

Spring was obviously in the air in April 1985 when I met some friends at the "soccer house" on the north end of campus. The soccer house wasn't an official designation; it was simply a small home on North Franklin Street where a number of the school's soccer team members resided. Soccer was a club sport at the time, not varsity, so it wasn't taken all that seriously. The house was legendary for its booze consumption.

The fraternity scene was lame for the most part, with just a small "Greek" population on campus, so most of the good stuff occurred at random house parties between campus and downtown Mt. Pleasant.

To get to the area, my housemates and I had to travel about two miles. We lived in a brand-spanking-new apartment complex called Chippewa Village, about three-quarters of a mile west of campus. It was townhouse style, each unit with its own private entrance, and we lived in A-1. They were all three-storey, five-bedroom bachelor or bachelorette pads, overlooking a central courtyard. Other pals from Thorpe Hall, our jock dorm down the street where we previously lived, also got past the waiting list and had hip pads at Chip' Village. Scott Smith, or "Smitty," whom I rode with to the party on the night of the theft, had the bedroom next to me on the top floor.

I don't remember whom I drank with, whom I chatted with, or for how long I stayed at the soccer house that April night. I'm sure it was a combination of the semi-regulars I hung out with and some randoms; all I know is that the proceedings got very liquid. But I somehow remember the remainder of the night, after I left the party, like it was yesterday.

Smitty was long gone by the time I started stumbling home at about three o'clock in the morning. The CMU campus is flat and rather cozy. The soccer house sat just a few doors up from Bellows Street, which runs across the north end of campus. It's only about a mile and a quarter south to Broomfield Street, which runs along the south end. Preston Street splits the difference, running parallel to the others, just a little north of centre. Just off Preston, in the heart of the campus, is where old Alumni Field sat.

I was a few steps north of the ballpark, meandering my way south, when I suddenly convinced myself I had to take a little piece of CMU baseball home with me. I mean, c'mon, in my mind I was the next Ernie Harwell (Detroit Tigers legendary broadcaster), and if things stayed the way they were, I'd be the first kid ever to broadcast Chippewa baseball as the main play-by-play guy for three (and then four) years, starting as a sophomore. Baseball broadcasting was my life. It was only my junior year, but I had to have the large memento right then. In my sloshed mind, I had to give myself an early twenty-first birthday present.

Stealing that sign is the perfect example of an item literally being "ripped off." It wasn't easy.

Had I been caught, years three and four of my CMU broadcasting career likely never would have happened. On top of the impending theft itself, I was carrying a couple cans of beer as I proceeded to the scene of the crime: open beer on campus, yet another infraction. Logic, utter embarrassment, arrest, possible secondary discipline of all kinds, my future — none of this seemed to enter my mind as I sipped my cold frothy outside the ballpark down the left-field line. In my enthusiastically devious, plastered mind, this outfield sign would forever make a delightful wall hanging.

It should come as no surprise at this point, being a pathological dolt, that I then began to do my best Bluto Blutarsky imitation. Bent at the knees, wide stance, head on a swivel, arms in the ready-to-wrestle position, I hopped back and forth in semicircles while humming the related music.

"Do-do, do-DO, do-do-da-Dooooo." I would pretend to be John Belushi in *Animal House* at least three more times during my escape.

At almost six-foot-six, I had an advantage. I could easily reach up to the top of the fence that ran along the outside of the playing field and pull myself up, and I was in decent enough shape to do so. But it was still going to require a pretty solid effort, and I'd have to do it quickly to avoid being seen or heard. I knew I needed a really good burst, and I knew I could get scraped up pretty good or snap a leg. Call it drunken adrenaline: if I hadn't been loaded, I never would have tried it.

I grabbed the top of the fence, jumped, and pulled my head and shoulders up enough to get my right elbow on top of the barrier. I pushed off with my feet, shuffled them up, and lunged until half of my body was over and inside the fence and the other half was outside. I looked like a human teeter-totter. With the wood digging into my gut and my hands in an awkward and painful position, I instantly spun right, brought both feet around so I was parallel with the top, and then awkwardly swung both feet over and let go. I landed on the warning track in foul territory.

At that point, I wished I had brought one of the beers over the wall with me. It was a baseball paradise. I sat down, rested briefly, and stared out at the ball field, the evergreen trees that encircled part of it, the press box, and the stars above. I savoured the peacefulness of the diamond.

After a quick scan for car lights and people in the distance, I turned my attention to the sign. Surprisingly, I wasn't nervous. It was dark, there was obviously no one at or around the ballpark, and I was hidden in the extreme corner where the outfield fence met the barrier I had just scaled.

I stood face to face with the metal sign on a wooden fence, a maroon 325 on a gold background, with a maroon outline. And God Bless America, there were only two bolts. They were big, intimidating bolts, but instead of four, one in each corner, there were only two, one above and one below the middle digit.

Yank up, or yank down? I asked myself. I'd get more strength pulling down. *And do it quickly.* I grabbed the top of the sign with one hand on either side of the bolt and yanked. Nothing. "Shit!" This sucker was *on* the wall. I'd have to give it everything I had.

One, two, three, PULL! I yelled in my mind. The sign-bolt-and-fence made a hideous sound of metal on metal, metal on wood. But it moved. In fact, it moved enough so that the nut at the back end of the bolt had partially wedged into the fence. With the nut held in place, I was able to manoeuver the sign and unscrew the bolt by hand the rest of the way.

The sign spun down and around until it was upside down, with the lower bolt now at the top of the dangling sign. Using the leverage of the sign itself against the fence, I was able to pry the second bolt out of the wall.

Success on one hand, doubt on the other. *What the*

hell am I doing? I thought. I was at the point of no return. Leave it or take it?

I decided to go for it. I walked twenty feet along the fence towards home plate and with two hands, tossed the piece of sheet metal over the wall like a Frisbee. The six-pound sign, one-sixteenth of an inch thick, thirty inches long and two feet wide, landed without a clang. It landed upright on one of its corners with a thud, digging into the ground, and then fell over. I then walked back to the corner, thinking somehow I was distancing myself from the goods, before climbing up and out.

After a quick Belushi, I walked to the sign, picked it up, and began a nerve-racking mile-long walk home.

At times I jogged. Other times I walked very slowly. When a car came, I dropped the sign, walked away, only to return a few moments later. When another car came, as I crossed the western edge of campus, I pointed the sign at the vehicle lengthwise and followed the car's movement. I thought this way, if they looked at me, they'd have only a sixteenth of an inch of sign to notice. I proceeded cautiously across a well-lit parking lot and then through an open area along Crawford Road, behind CMU's largest dorm complex, the Towers.

I knew I was home free for the most part when I arrived at the woods that separated campus from a cluster of apartment complexes on the other side. I ran through the trail in the dark for an eighth of a mile. I hurried around and through a couple of complexes, scurried to Chip' Village, came along the empty courtyard, entered my dark apartment, and rushed upstairs. No one was awake. I zipped to the third floor, hopped into my room,

The now infamous sign.

and slid the sign between my mattress and my box spring. Mission accomplished.

You, I thought, *are an idiot*. But I was really happy I got the sign.

It wasn't long after this that I learned karma can be a bear. Cue John Lachance.

The same age as me, I believe, he was a big dude, almost as tall, six-foot-five or so and, I'd guess, about twenty or thirty pounds heavier. He was somewhat loud and extremely assertive, especially when it came to developing and solidifying his position as a student journalist in the CMU Broadcast and Cinematic Arts Department.

Lachance could be an intimidating figure, but he was as sweet as molasses when he approached me that spring and asked if he could join me for a couple of baseball broadcasts. I agreed, figuring it was no big deal, and rationalized that although I was the student "Voice of Chippewa Baseball," I had no right to deny another kid an opportunity, albeit a brief one.

We did a couple of games together with Central hosting the Bowling Green Falcons. I recall doing play-by-play for the first three innings and the final three, with him as my color commentator, and allowing him to do play-by-play for the middle three innings.

I still have the air-check tapes. At one point, I announced, ". . . checks the base runners and delivers . . . hit harrrd, base hit to right field past the first baseman . . . this should be two runs, Fisher rounds third, here comes the throw to the plate, he is safe at home! A two-run single for Bob Podschlne [pronounced Po-chell-knee] as he does the job, and the Chippewa lead is five to one." The cheers subsided a bit.

John's color: "Once again, Rob, let's go back, they got the first man . . . up, got him on the base." That was pretty much it. I then reviewed the rally hitter by hitter.

Shortly thereafter I said, "Kevin working with a four-run margin, his Chippewas have done a good job offensively today . . . the next onnnnne, just on the outside corner. The umpire seemed to take about ten seconds to make the call, but it's a two-two count now."

John: "That would be par for the day for him, wouldn't it be?"

The cool part for both of us was that we were watching a future major-leaguer pitch a complete-game victory for CMU. Chippewa ace Kevin Tapani blew through the Falcons line-up and racked up ten strikeouts with his ninety-four-mile-per-hour fastball.

Three years after his senior-year no-hitter against Eastern Michigan in 1986, "Tap" made his major-league debut on July 4, 1989, for the Mets against the Astros. After a trade to Minnesota a year later, he went on to help win a World Series for Minnesota in 1991 and was a workhorse starter in the bigs for thirteen seasons. In 1999, he was elected to the CMU Athletics Hall of Fame, joining other baseball honorees like Tom Tresh, Chris Knapp, and Curt Young.

When the weekend was all said and done, I thought, *Well, that's one less competitor for any future play-by-play gigs, that's for sure.*

Au contraire.

Lachance moved along, and I did the rest of the season on my own or with my eventual regular sidekick Rick Maklebust. He was a nice kid, with a good set of pipes, and it was a delightful spring. We had the opportunity to improve our craft and hang around the ballpark and talk baseball.

As the season slipped toward summer, there was only one date remaining on the calendar that meant anything to any of the kids in the broadcast department: the spring meeting for the fall football telecasts.

CMU football games were handled top-to-bottom by an all-student crew on the campus television station, which at that time was a rare opportunity. Central was a top-notch regional broadcasting school and one of the best in the nation for actual hands-on vocational opportunities. Longtime NBC Sportscaster Dick Enberg, who attended CMU as an undergrad before getting his masters at Indiana, was our poster boy.

A couple of weeks later, the football meeting arrived. Two or three dozen students eagerly took their seats in a large lecture auditorium in Anspach Hall. It had shaped up to be an exciting time for each and every young broadcast student, whether one planned on being a cameraperson, a runner, a tape guy or gal, a producer, or, in my case, the clear choice to handle play-by-play. But it was at that meeting that a bombshell fell into my young broadcasting life, and I learned a hard lesson about how things would eventually work in the real world.

Filling talent positions sometimes has very little to do with talent.

When the meeting began, the instructor who ran the television side of the broadcast department, Greydon Hyde, took the stage as expected. The appearance of Lachance close alongside was a shock to all of us.

They distributed handouts, including an outline of production plans and a list of jobs. Students could rank, one through three, what they were interested in, with "most interested in" being number one and "less interested in" being number two and then three. Producer was a popular one, as was camera operator for those more interested in the technical side. Oddly, "play-by-play" wasn't listed, just color commentator.

Then the announcement: John Lachance was the student executive producer or coordinating producer AND play-by-play guy. He had essentially named himself to the crème-de-la-crème position. Hyde made the announcement.

How the hell had Lachance pulled this off? Ass-kissing? Intimidation? Had they become drinking buddies? Had Lachance used, "I did some baseball games," to convince Hyde to give him the gig? As Maklebust and I looked over at one another, our mouths agape from shock, the overwhelming sentiment was "What the fuck?"

So there it was. Pissed off, sick to my stomach, in disbelief. What was I gonna do about it? That was the true, gigantic question.

Option one: stand-up and say, "How the hell did this guy give himself the play-by-play job and why is there no audition? I want at least a fair crack at this thing. Are you freaking kidding me?" Or at least something along those lines.

Option two: sit, squirm, stew, and say nothing.

Sadly, I chose option two. I never complained and, soon after, it was case closed once summer break arrived.

I actually ended up taking the color commentary job and sat with Lachance in the booth as he did play-by-play. He pretty much sounded exactly like a college student broadcaster doing college football play-by-play. Maybe that was the point of the whole thing. Maybe it *was* time to give someone else a shot. I just didn't like the way I think he went about it.

For the second game of the season, against Bowling Green, we actually shared the telecast with a professional regional broadcast group, with longtime Detroit sportscasting stalwart Dave Diles doing play-by-play on a separate broadcast feed. Lachance, being in on the planning, managed to get the lone student position, sideline reporter, for that regional telecast.

With Lachance out of the box, I jumped over and did play-by-play for our local market. My one chance to do what I thought I deserved to do in the first place, and my one chance to hopefully get a decent demo tape.

But that was pretty much it for me. I didn't go passive-aggressive with the whole situation; I went passive-passive. After three games, I quit and handed off the color gig to Maklebust. My handling of the whole scenario showed just how immature, naïve, and unprepared I was for the real deal. In this case, just like in other businesses, personal politics (or ethnicity, or age, or gender, or aesthetics), often factor in more than knowledge and ability. It's a fact a young broadcaster needs to prepare for. Never expect or assume anything.

At that point, I turned the rest of my CMU career into a holiday. I was, as we used to say a lot back then, "over it."

That school year I had landed the operations manager job at the student radio station, 91-Rock-FM. It was essentially the top student executive position. I think I showed up for two of the twenty-six weekly board meetings. I bagged out of air shifts, I went to class when I had to, I caroused and chased coeds. I was a child. I had acute fifth-year senioritis. By the time June 1986 rolled around, I had a diploma, I had training, I had my talent and ability, I had a sense of what to expect in the real world, and I had one very large, metal memento.

The outfield is still symmetrical at the new ballpark called Bill Theunissen Stadium in Mt. Pleasant, but it's now 330 feet down the foul lines. So I guess they're not missing the 325 marker. It's been put to practical use only once, on the outfield fence of a Wiffle ball field on Nantucket.

John Lachance persevered in another side of the business. He's apparently been at ESPN since 2004 and he's reached a senior executive operations position. He didn't return my voice messages.

"Um, Roger . . . you're naked."

———

**Me, to my golf pro,
January 1996**

THE FORBIDDEN ISLE

There are actually thousands of Hawaiian islands, referred to as the Northwest Hawaiian Islands, essentially made up of bird sanctuaries and volcanic pop-ups that stretch more than a thousand miles through the Pacific Ocean. At the bottom of this archipelago sit the eight largest islands that make up the state of Hawaii.

Ask any American to name the eight main Hawaiian Islands and he or she would probably be able to name two: Hawaii and Maui. Okay, maybe one: Hawaii. And they'd think they were naming the island where the capital city of Honolulu is located (if they didn't also incorrectly guess that Honolulu is an island itself).

I point this out because Americans, unlike Canadians, are typically, dramatically, disturbingly, and sadly geographically challenged, even when it comes to their own country. Hey, can you name the capital of Oregon? Didn't think so. How about the five Great Lakes?

Not that Hawaii has anything to do with the rest of the country, thankfully, other than falling under the same legal and institutional umbrella. It's a wondrous, intricate, naturally spiritual land that operates very much on its own. Until 120-odd years ago, it was its own sovereign kingdom, stolen by the United States and later made a territory and then a state for economic and military purposes.

Hawaii's capital city is on the island of Oahu, which in Hawaiian means "the gathering place." It houses about three-quarters of the state's population, a dynamic mixture of Japanese, Chinese, Portuguese, Samoan, Filipino, Korean, other non-native Hawaiians, and American Caucasians, the latter also known as mainland *haole* (how-lee).

The weather is close to perfect more often than not, with the northeasterly trade winds blowing 80 percent of the time; the topography is absolutely gorgeous; and there is a disproportionately large number of excruciatingly beautiful female inhabitants. The term "paradise" likely has as much to do with this last feature as it does with the mountains, the cliffs, the flowers, the trees, the waterfalls, the beaches, and the weather.

The island of Hawaii itself is indeed one of the eight main islands in the chain, but it's known locally as "The

Big Island," as it's the largest. It's also the only one with an active volcano, Kilauea (Kill-ow-A-ah). Between the sometimes snow-capped, almost 14,000-foot peak of Mauna Kea to the north and the more rounded Mauna Loa to the south (shorter by 115 feet) lies the saddle, a ridge of land that eventually connects the town of Hilo on the windward side to Kona on the drier leeward side.

East, west, north, and south are somewhat meaningless geographic labels in Hawaii, outside of South Point, the southernmost point of the Big Island and of the United States. The islands are generally round with mountainous interiors, so when one moves towards the ocean from inland, they travel *makai* (ma-kye), and when they head inland from the water they're going *mauka* (mow-ka, rhymes with cow-ka), towards the mountains. Similarly, instead of west or east, one moves towards or away from a prominent landmark, as the circular nature of shoreline travel dictates. In Honolulu, for example, you move "Diamond Head" or "Koko Head," in the direction of those extinct volcanoes along the shore; or you move in the opposite direction, Ewa (Eva), towards Ewa Beach.

Maui is well known to many because it's the second most visited island by tourists and is referred to more frequently in pop culture than the other islands, as in "Maui Wowee," a reference to pot. Really good pot is known as *da kine*, as is anything else that's accepted as local knowledge, very good, or right on. Don't worry, I didn't inhale. (I say that because I, along with a few hundred other people on Waikiki Beach in 1994, actually shook hands with President Clinton, the most famous "non-inhaler.")

Besides Oahu, Maui, and Hawaii, the other inhabited

islands are Kauai, Lanai, and Molokai. Kauai, "The Garden Isle," furthest north, is home to some places of startling beauty, including Waimea Canyon. Picture a smaller, logic-defyingly green version of the Grand Canyon. Lanai and Molokai sit in the middle of the island group and are polar opposites in terms of their development, despite both being lightly inhabited. Molokai, "The Friendly Isle," is truly that — very local and goes to sleep when the sun goes down. Lanai, formerly a Dole Company–owned pineapple plantation before its operations and jobs went to Mexico, is now privately owned by an American media mogul. It has one delightful, high-end resort on the coast and another one up in the misty mountains. In the early 1990s, Bill Gates rented the entire island for his wedding.

Which leaves us with the two islands no mainland American can name, practically or literally, Kahoolawe (Ka-ho-oh-la-vay) and Niihau (Nee-ee-how). Kahoolawe is uninhabited because it's believed there is still un-exploded military ordnance on it, as in navy bombs that were dropped and didn't blow up. For decades, the U.S. military used this island just a few miles off the south coast of Maui as a bombing range. It's the only island of the group I never visited.

I made it to seven of the eight because I was blessed to visit Niihau, "The Forbidden Isle," as part of a January 1996 experience I could never have dreamed up. My then-wife, Nora, bought me the unexpected trip as a Christmas present for about $250. That was a very expensive gift for us in those days and, ultimately, it proved to be a priceless one. I had moved to Hawaii to work at the CBS affiliate in 1991, and I would be leaving for good in less than two weeks. At that point in history, very few non-Niihauans or non-ancient Hawaiian warriors had ever set foot on the island. Our opportunity to go there arose because the island's owners were looking for a way to help pay their hefty federal estate taxes.

A woman named Elizabeth Sinclair bought Niihau and some land on Kauai from King Kamehameha I in the 1860s. Sinclair's descendants, Bruce and Keith Robinson, still own it. They've apparently turned down offers of as much as a billion dollars for Niihau; their steadfast intent is to keep it pristine and intact for the native Hawaiians who live there. In 2010, the population was listed as 170.

The excursion I made was offered starting in about 1992 but was hardly publicized, nor were the private safari expeditions to hunt boar. The Robinsons wanted to find any way they could to chip away at their debt to the U.S. government, but I don't think they were really enthused about inviting tourists. We were lucky and privileged to discover the opportunity locally.

Having been fully indoctrinated into, and appreciative of, the Aloha Spirit, "one with the *aina* ['land']," if you will, I can't properly describe the anticipation I felt for this day trip. Truly like a small child on Christmas morning. More accurately like a man-child, full of wonder and wanderlust, taking a really cool next step in a life of travel and exploration.

My wife didn't want to spend *another* $250, nor did she have the same interest in visiting Niihau. So whom would I share this adventure with?

Not that long before Roger Fredericks became the king of golf exercise and swing instruction videos, he ran the Delmar Golf School at the Sheraton Makaha on the leeward side of Oahu. He and his girlfriend/assistant had moved to the islands in the early 1990s from San Diego. He was a great instructor with a big problem: no one was really going to the Sheraton Makaha on the leeward side of Oahu. As local TV sports guys, my fellow KGMB-TV sports anchor, Scott Culbertson, and I tried to pump up his business a little bit with publicity and features about the school. Over time, we became buds with Roger and he gave us some helpful golf lessons I still utilize today.

A great guy in general, Roger is a bit quirky. Goofy. His odd sense of humour became a popular element in his golf instruction videos. He would later incorporate yoga into his exercise, stretching, and golf programs as well, although I didn't have any idea he was into yoga until we arrived on Niihau.

Roger was game for whatever Hawaiian adventures came his way. For example, when I skydived for the first time, Roger came along and also jumped out of the airplane over the North Shore of Oahu. As he fell, he had one arm out where it was supposed to be, but his other hand was on top of his head. The footage from the videographer, falling at the same speed and shooting back at him, shows Roger plummeting to Earth while trying to hold in place whatever portion of his hair wasn't naturally his.

Sounds odd, but the other participant in our adventure that day on Niihau was Neil Everett's ex-wife, Mary. Neil was our backup weekend sports anchor and the dude I spent the most time hanging out with during my last two years in Hawaii. We were both sports nuts who gambled casually on a regular basis. We'd get together to drink beer and watch college football or basketball games from the east coast at two in the afternoon. (Hawaii doesn't do the daylight savings crap, so Honolulu is five hours behind New York in winter and six hours behind in the summer.) My wife worked until five. Neil and I had a couple of regular spots including Club Sun in Honolulu, kind of a combination sports bar/Korean strip club. There was always someone to look at during the commercials.

I have forgotten the names of many an establishment over the years, but I'll never forget the name Club Sun.

In early January 1996, my next-to-last week in Hawaii, a day after we had met with him to go over my little going-away shindig the following weekend, Club Sun's owner, Andy, was shot dead behind the bar. The two gunmen didn't take any money. They walked in, shot him, and walked out. Andy was either into some shady shit and pissed off the wrong guy, *or*, he was just a regular guy who chose the wrong business.

Neil and I went to his Buddhist funeral a few days later. The venue was packed. We walked by Andy's body to pay our respects. Most of the people were chanting the same thing over and over the entire time. It was trippy.

Neil and I did a lot of cool stuff exploring Oahu — kayaking, cruising around town, attending sporting events — and we briefly hosted a weekly radio show together. Unfortunately, he had to miss my wedding because someone had to fill in for me on the weekend sportscast.

Neil couldn't make Niihau. Maybe he couldn't afford it. But he said his ex-wife, Mary, would absolutely love to go.

Roger and I met at the Honolulu airport and flew to

Our helicopter on Niihau. At one point it had been repainted and used in the film *Jurassic Park*.

Kauai. We met Mary at an airstrip in Hanapepe (Ha-na-pay-pay). The fourth participant on the trip was a random Englishman in his sixties. It was kind of weird — we never spoke to the guy.

Not long before our excursion, Steven Spielberg had wrapped up shooting a little flick on Kauai called *Jurassic Park*. We'd be flying in the helicopter that had been repainted and used as the park helicopter in the movie. Spielberg apparently had also used it for his personal transportation around the island while he was in production. We felt special.

We lifted off and headed pretty much due west for the trip to Niihau, with no idea where exactly we were going or what to expect. It's only about twenty miles from the western side of Kauai to Niihau via canoe, but almost fifty miles from where we took off to where we would touch down for the first time.

We swung past cliffs on the east side of Niihau at Pueo (Poo-eh-oh) Point and headed southwest. The cliffs gave way to pristine beaches along the coast and mostly dry, thick brush in the interior. We crossed over the island and landed near an area called Kamalino. So thrilled were we fucking *haoles*, we actually all got down on our hands and knees and kissed the *aina*. Giddy exclamations and comments followed.

"We're here!"

"This is unreal."

"I never thought I'd be on Niihau."

Lying on the beach nearby was a rare Hawaiian monk seal.

Ten minutes later, we were back in the chopper and headed north. We flew right over the lone village of Puuwai (Poo-oo-why), which sits exactly halfway up the island along the west coast. No, there weren't grass or mud huts, but they were very simple wooden dwellings. We continued north along the coastline until Niihau ended. The pilot circled us around the steep sides of Lehua (Lay-who-ah), a separate volcanic half-cone islet sitting a short distance from Niihau's north shore. It was literally breathtaking. I dreamed we could land on it, explore, and snorkel inside the waters of the crescent-shaped bay on the north side. Instead, we circled back and landed at the very northern end of Niihau, on the beach at Keamano (Kay-ah-mon-oh) Bay.

The pilot pulled out a picnic lunch: sandwiches and juice boxes. We ate, stared out across a massive, untouched beach that stretched a mile to the next point, and marvelled. The next thing I knew, Roger had wandered off, as had Mary, in opposite directions. The English dude shot the shit with the pilot while I just kicked back for a bit and then walked to the water. I couldn't take my eyes off Lehua, the back side of it looming just off to our left.

Mary returned with a skull. Knowing the history, familiar with the Hawaiian traditions and the taboos, I immediately got nervous.

"Um, not a great idea," I said.

It was the skull of a human child and, based on my very limited paleontological skills, looked to be at least a hundred years old. The Hawaiians often buried their dead in the sand dunes. She set it aside with every intention of taking it home with her, like some type of tourist artifact. I wasn't about to lecture or explain why, but I knew that wasn't going to happen. I walked away from what was a mini buzz-kill.

Thirty yards away on the beach was a Hawaiian war canoe, left behind in the late 1790s when King Kamehameha I came from the big island and tried to conquer Niihau and unify all the islands. It didn't go so well. His warriors got slaughtered. Eventually the islands all came together as a Hawaiian kingdom through marriage and more peaceful means.

The canoe was in fantastic condition, which made sense, because hardly any human beings had set foot on this beach since the vessel arrived. No one in our group ventured very far into the thick brush that surrounded the beaches for two main reasons. One, we were standing on an untouched, perfect, incredibly beautiful beach; and two, no one was carrying a gun in case we ran into a wild boar.

This was a "lie around and appreciate your surroundings and maybe take a dip or two" visit. Which brings us to Roger.

I set off to find him. Mary followed after a few minutes and gradually caught up to me. We were walking east, from Puukola (Poo-oo-cola) Point at one end of the bay towards the other end at Kikepa (Kee-kay-pa) Point. Near Kikepa we could see another ancient canoe on the beach with a little human head popping up and down on the other side of it. This head was still alive. It was Roger, doing some stretching and yoga moves in the sand — while buck-naked.

"One with the *aina*."

Mary had stopped to check out some shells along the water, so I arrived on the scene first. This allowed Roger time to pull on his shorts.

"Oops, sorry," he said, laughing when he noticed Mary nearby.

"Dude, no worries." Like it really mattered.

Mary smiled and appreciated the fact that Roger had felt inspired and comfortable enough to let it all hang out. Seriously, it was Niihau, we were the only human beings on a mile-long stretch of beach that had probably seen ten other Caucasians in its history. Who cares and why not? But we didn't strip down to join him *au naturel*. I might have made that suggestion if we hadn't been with Neil's ex-wife, but instead we went for a swim and took wicked-cool album-cover style photographs of ourselves doing staggered yoga positions on the beach. Shorts and bikini on, or shorts and bikini off, it didn't matter; we were relishing what time we had left in one of the most unique places on the planet.

Quite a contrast in perspective compared to my first month on the islands in 1991. I was new at the TV station, as was a local Japanese camera guy named John. We were both sent to the leeward side of Oahu to do a story about someone wanting to construct a building on top of a *heiau* (hey-yow). *Heiau* are sacred places, temples, or Hawaiian remains of significance. While John and I were looking for the *heiau*, stumbling around an area of uneven ground near the beach, a dude kindly pulled up.

I go, "Hey man, do you know where the *heiau* is?"

And he goes, "Yeah, bruddah, you're walking all over it."

Oh shit.

We were in Waianea (Why-a-nye) in the heart of the leeward side, about as badass local as it gets. Fortunately, no one stopped to kick our ass or give us too much grief. Red-faced, we thanked the guy, moved along quickly, and got on with making our news story. Ever since, I have been a master of *heiau* respect and etiquette. It's quite simple: don't fuck with *heiau*.

By Niihau, I had a come a long way emotionally and intellectually since I had arrived in Hawaii four years earlier. My appreciation for the culture and customs, both modern and ancient, ran deep. I learned to diss the politics of life, to not sweat the bullshit, and to relax.

I had a unique opportunity to learn the customs and the culture of Hawaii, to interview people about them, to talk to remarkable people from all walks of life, and to travel extensively on seven of the eight islands. I was a broadcaster who was given extraordinary opportunities. And I was a broadcaster who wasn't a dick.

The amazing experience that was Niihau was almost over, but not quite. We reluctantly made our way back to Spielberg's chopper. "Leave nothing but your footprints behind and take away only memories" is a philosophy of respect in such unspoiled and spiritual places, and it kicked in beautifully with the help of our pilot. As I expected, when Mary suggested bringing the skull along as a keepsake, our guide was having nothing to do with it.

"Not a chance. You have to put that back." Thank you, helicopter man.

Roger hopped aboard, fully clothed and absolutely delighted with the experience — spiritually touched and repetitively thankful. It was cool. I was really happy he so appreciated the opportunity.

On the trip back to Kauai, a Niihau native and his young son joined us and sat in the front seat next to the pilot. I didn't know it then, but locals are occasionally shuttled over to Kauai to pick up supplies or visit relatives or whatever. The man didn't speak to us; the boy never even gave us a look. The four of us *haoles* sat in the back of the helicopter and looked out the windows as Niihau became smaller in the distance.

I watched the man and his son for any type of reaction or communication. I found it fascinating. Had either one of them been off the island before? I doubted the kid had. Where were they going? Does the boy speak English or Hawaiian? Is he completely freaked out by the white people in the back seat? Has he ever seen a white person?

So many questions and thoughts entered my mind because having them along was so unexpected. I wasn't going to say a word to them. To me, they were like royalty in a way. I didn't want to tarnish their existence or experience.

Just riding in a helicopter with native Hawaiians, a rich and thriving culture in its purest form just 125 years ago, but now almost extinct — the significance of the moment will never be lost.

In recent years, the Robinsons have solved their whopping tax problem by allowing the U.S. military to set up various electronic equipment on Niihau. As far as I know, it's remote, there's no weaponry, and they're not allowed interaction with the locals.

Neil Everett has been working at ESPN as a sports anchor since 2000, after having his talents discovered while working at our TV station in Hawaii. He's happily remarried. He's a brother from another mother.

And in case you're still curious, the capital of Oregon is Salem and the five Great Lakes are Ontario, Erie, Huron, Michigan, and Superior.

Check out your anchor boy on YouTube: Simpson Hawaii Anchor

THE SWAMP

In 1979, while still only midway through our Fundamentals in Radio Broadcasting class in high school, my best friend, Ric Blackwell, and I decided to form Simpwell Productions. Simp' would be the chairman of the board and 'Well would be the president. We established a handshake: the standard everyday grip, followed by our simultaneous re-enactment of a lunging basketball referee bringing his arm around over his head and "counting the basket." It's a handshake still in use almost forty years later.

We were playing make-believe business with Simpwell, but we were also very serious and determined. After redefining the quality of high-school radio with a show called *Sportscan*, with guests from the NBA, NHL, and local television actually visiting us in-studio, we earned some ink (thanks in part to some urgent lobbying from 'Well).

Instant Replay column, Jay Mariotti, *The Detroit News*, Thursday, November 5, 1981:

> Yep, another talk show. I received a phone call yesterday from Ric Blackwell of radio station WBFH-FM in Bloomfield Hills.
>
> "We'd like you to publicize our talk show," said Blackwell.
>
> Fine. Ric Blackwell and another fellow, Rob Simpson, host a weekly sports talk show on WBFH every Wednesday night from 6 to 8. Blackwell and Simpson are seniors at Bloomfield Hills Andover High School. The station is a 10-watt community outlet associated with Andover High and Lahser High. Sophomores at both schools can enroll in a course, Fundamentals of Radio Broadcasting. The students are then placed in a position at the radio station. Sports, it seems, is the most popular area.
>
> "We've got a large staff," Blackwell said. "Our school's football and basketball games are handled by Rob and myself, but we have other students doing volleyball, hockey, baseball, and junior-high sports."

Among their guests on the talk show have been Gordie Howe, Al Kaline, and Channel 4 sportscaster Eli Zaret.

"Personally, my two favourites in the Detroit market are Don Shane [another guest] and Eli," Blackwell said. "They're fresh and something new for the area. It's not the same old routine with them."

Blackwell and Simpson will attend Central Michigan University. Upon graduation in 1986, they should be ready to replace Anne Doyle and Jim Price on Channel 2's weekend charade.

Actually, Doyle and Price were bad enough I think we could have replaced them right out of high school. Price was a former backup catcher for the Tigers and Doyle was the daughter of local radio sports fixture Vince Doyle. It might have been the worst example of "ex-jockism" and market nepotism in the history of sports television.

Unfortunately, Ric and I weren't quite ready to take over in 1986. Especially considering Ric didn't get out of CMU until December 1986, and I stayed on for the five-year plan. After that, I dicked around and travelled for a while.

By August 1990, Ric was pulling most of the weight in our young broadcasting careers. After hooking me up with a news gig in Tuscaloosa, Alabama, the year before, Ric was trying to get me a job in Florida. Instead of a friend and colleague, Ric could have been my agent. He was finding me work when I wasn't even looking for it.

"Get down here, I'm moving to night beat reporter

Simpwell Productions — Rob Simpson and
Ric Blackwell — at the 1991 Gator Bowl in
Jacksonville, Florida. Michigan 35, Mississippi 3.

at WINK-TV and they're looking for someone to fill my
bureau-chief spot. Send tape," he advised.

I sent tape, the news director liked it, and two weeks
later, I moved further south. After eleven months in Dixie,
the Fort Myers/Naples market came calling.

Florida is a strange state full of strange people. Besides
the small percentage of natives, and the smaller percentage
of "cracker" cowboys (pioneer frontiersmen who moved
to the remote south to work the land), most of the population is made up of two types of immigrants: old snow-
birds from up north, and Latinos from the Caribbean. Of
course, there's yet another niche of the population: dangerous drifters.

I first saw a mangled body in Florida. I first saw a burned body and I first smelled death there too. The odour of a dead body and its residue, especially outdoors in ninety-five-degree heat, is unforgettable, and may just be the nastiest smell in existence.

In one gruesome Charlotte County incident, two homophobes decided to kill a gay man. They forced him to drink engine coolant, stuffed a rag down his throat, then cut off his penis and threw it in the Peace River. Just in case he wasn't dead yet, they set him on fire. Police found his body in a field a week later.

After they removed the body, I decided to head to the site to shoot video and perform an on-camera stand-up.

Normally, as a "one-man-band," acting as reporter *and* cameraman, stand-ups were a big enough pain in the ass. If I wanted to appear in a story, I had to shoot myself. This involved picking a place to stand or squat, guesstimating the shot through the viewfinder, pushing Record, running in front of the camera, positioning myself, running back, rewinding the tape, and checking the video to see if I fit in the frame correctly. If I did, fine, I'd hit Record again, go to the spot, and talk to the camera. If not, I'd adjust based on what the practice shot revealed, and then try it again.

In the case of the dead body, it was especially gnarly. I could see the imprint where the body had rested in the weeds. Flies swarmed on and around the residue on the ground. To go with the stench, as I knelt next to the spot, the flies swarmed on me. I felt like I was in the Australian outback; flies were in my eyes, on my nose, all while I was trying to speak. I managed the stand-up in two takes.

But dead bodies would not be my greatest test of puke

retention. Being on a lengthy peninsula with hundreds of miles of saltwater shoreline, it seemed inevitable that I'd find myself on the water.

I possessed little fear. In my previous travels, I had crossed a stormy English Channel, a wavy Bass Strait between the Australian mainland and the island state of Tasmania, a temperamental Nantucket Sound, and a rough-and-tumble Lake Michigan. Never once had I experienced seasickness.

However, I had also never been on any of those bodies of water while looking through a video-camera viewfinder. It's a game changer, and for myself and many others, it makes riding the ocean blue a whole different experience.

On April 29, 1991, I headed for the Mote Marine Laboratory on Longboat Key, off Sarasota. This would be my first-ever story on sharks. The world-renowned laboratory was promoting its annual "catch-and-release" shark tournament. Big-game fishermen would have the opportunity to perfect their craft and revel in the chance to catch a monster shark, all in the name of science.

The lab benefitted because the fishermen were, in essence, working for research. Some of the sharks would be held and studied, while most would be tagged and unhooked to be released back into the wild. It was the perfect example of two generally opposite entities working on a mutually beneficial endeavour.

Boasting my unscathed record on the sea, I hopped on one of the press boats with seven other people for the tournament preview. Two reporters from Sarasota continuously expressed concern about seasickness. The captain and I attempted to reassure them.

"Just look at the horizon," we advised. "Keep moving around. Don't sit down inside the cabin. You'll be fine."

The journey would take us about four miles out into the Gulf, to a zone considered somewhat infested with sharks. Two fishing boats followed. My job included shooting video of people on the other vessels attempting to catch sharks.

For two minutes of work, I didn't notice a thing. I took shots of our captain, the other boats, the wake, and what I thought were dramatic shots of the wavy seas. Two minutes later, I was overcome. Rocking back and forth while looking through the viewfinder with my other eye closed did wacky things to my gut.

The afternoon's drama was now taking place in my belly. I'm pretty sure I've never felt worse.

I left the crowd at the open area astern and took my camera along the narrow starboard side to the bow. There I could be alone for a few moments under the guise of busy TV photographer.

Wrong! When I reached the front of the boat, I found a young lady already in anguish. She vomited repeatedly off the port side.

Soon, the ocean claimed its second victim. I felt that irrepressible feeling. The boat rocked. Moments later, half of the Dr Pepper I had for breakfast came shooting out my pursed mouth and swollen nostrils and hit the deck. Oh, the sting of carbonation.

"Ahhh, much better," I said, drawing in a deep breath. Best of all, I had gacked in private, as the sick girl remained with her head flung over the side. I just prayed the active sea spray would quickly wash away my modest amount of yack.

For ten minutes, my bravado survived intact; my brush with mortality on the high seas remained undetected. I proceeded to the back of the boat to shoot more video.

Twenty seconds after my face hit the viewfinder, my liquid breakfast mounted a second attack. The carbonated "Doctor" was not happy staying cooped up; he simply had to get out.

The hurling and the dry heaves that followed my second trip to the bow left me queasy for the next twenty minutes. My photographer chores, at least those *on* the water, had come to an abrupt conclusion. I stayed up front for the return journey to the harbour.

The second my feet hit the dock, I regained my legs and felt like a million dollars.

"It was the soda I had for breakfast. I was in a hurry and didn't eat anything. Big mistake," I explained to the curious and beautiful young TV reporter from Sarasota.

"Oh, well, as long as you feel better now, let's grab some lunch," she replied enthusiastically.

No, really, let's stay here and talk a little more about puke, I said to myself as she walked away. *I don't know how this is working out, but I like it.*

Actually, a fat ham sandwich was exactly what I needed. I ate with vigour. The rest of the day, I shot video of sharks in tanks and interviewed scientists and fishermen and smiled at the "hottie" reporter. Not one shark had been caught during our media adventure.

"Sucks, same thing happened last year," our captain

explained. "We get the media here, it's choppy, and no one catches a damn thing. I hope the tournament goes a hell of a lot better."

"I hope so too, Captain," I said. "I hope so too."

I spent thirteen months at WINK-TV, covering tropical storms, drug raids, murder cases, and disease epidemics, but the biggest calamity occurred just two minutes from my door.

During the whole time I lived in an apartment in Charlotte Harbor, just north of the Peace River, I spent maybe three Friday nights entirely at home. This particular Friday happened to be one of them.

I arrived home from an evening story at about 7:30 p.m. and fell asleep. I had just sat through an important but boring public hearing on funding for local emergency medical services. Residents argued that local bureaucrats shouldn't cut the EMS budget. The county commissioners used a full two hours of rhetoric to agree. On a Friday night!

The meeting was prophetic. I hadn't seen or heard the last of EMS for the evening.

I awoke in a daze about midnight, at first thinking it was time to get up and drive to Fort Myers for a WINK golf outing. I saw the clock and quickly settled in to go back to sleep. As I lay in bed, contemplating putts, chips, and bogeys, I heard the wailing approach of a fire engine.

Living off Farnam Street, a couple blocks from US 41, I often heard the sounds of emergency vehicles, and from frequent exposure to sirens, I could distinguish a patrol car from an ambulance, an ambulance from a fire engine or hook and ladder. I always knew when to give chase and when to relax. If in doubt, I'd flip on my police scanner.

This night, I heard the sounds of all four. Less than a minute after the fire engine, two patrol cars whizzed past my neighbourhood onto the southbound Peace River Bridge. After another thirty seconds, an ambulance. Then more police cars, then another ambulance. The screaming vehicles began to drown out one another.

As I listened, I ran out my front door and stood in front of my WINK-mobile. A herd of emergency vehicles thundered across the river.

"Damn! This is a big one." I ran inside.

Two thoughts entered my mind as I threw on a shirt and yanked on my blue jeans. First, some big building has gone up in flames. Second, this story was mine, mine, mine. My two Charlotte County bureau chief competitors wouldn't have a clue. Evan Bacon from WEVU-TV would probably be out and about and, if he wasn't, his apartment near I-75 was too far away to hear the action. The WBBH bureau chief commuted from Fort Myers, thirty-five miles south.

Whatever was going on, I'd have the exclusive.

It took only three minutes to grab my camera, hop in the car, and speed across the bridge.

I was surprised and almost relieved to see all of the police cars, fire vehicles, and ambulances sitting out in front of the Holiday Inn just south of the bridge. I wouldn't have to search around town for the fire. Time searching meant potential video time wasted.

As it turns out, it wasn't a fire at all. That night, I'd be covering the aftermath of an unusual and devastating explosion. At least a dozen people at the hotel dance club suffered flesh wounds and abrasions, two or three would be scarred, while one man lost a leg. All this happened while people were dancing: cuttin' the rug one moment, cut down the next.

The band had set up metal pipes full of pyrotechnics close to the front of their stage. Pyrotechnics, when handled and prepared properly, provide controlled explosions that blow upward just at the right moment. When the band hits the big note, the "light show" adds the perfect drama and excitement.

On this night, the pyrotechnics malfunctioned, literally exploding, sending shrapnel into walls, through ceiling panels, and into the limbs and torsos of patrons.

With the intensity of the explosions and the damage caused by the shrapnel, most witnesses couldn't believe there was no death.

Port Charlotte resident Scott Jones suffered the worst injury. The blast ripped off his right leg below the knee and severely damaged his left. He knew members of the band and had been standing close to the stage watching the revelry. Injured dancers collapsed nearby. A few of the partiers rushed forward to offer help while others ran in terror. Jones lay in a pool of his own blood.

The rescue efforts were ten minutes old when I had arrived. I set up my camera with the attached portable light and hoisted it on my shoulder. The police wouldn't let me inside, so I began the search out front for a quick explanation. As I picked up bits and pieces of the story from bystanders, I shot all of the outdoor "cover," or video of the scene, that I could. Five ambulances lined the hotel's driveway. One by one, they'd take victims to a nearby hospital, return, and get back in line.

Bottom line, particularly as time wore on, I desperately needed people to tell the dramatic story on camera. Without them, it would be hollow. Gathering no sound bites at a story like this would be incomprehensible and inexcusable.

Problem: a man carrying a video camera during a time of great emotion and trauma is nothing but a prick, a vulture. Many witnesses would have nothing to do with me. Many others, including all of my cop and fire buddies, were too busy with the rescue efforts.

Finally, in the parking lot, about fifteen rows from the front of the building, I found a willing interview subject: a drunken tourist from Boston.

"Oh, it was terrible. An explosion, really horrendous," he slurred thoughtfully. "It looked bad, a lot of injuries, a lot of blood." He paused and looked back at the hotel. "I think one guy lost his leg."

Thank God for drunken tourists from Boston. I had the momentum to continue unabashed.

Punta Gorda Police Public Information Officer (PIO) Naomi Patterson played a little hard to get. Our working relationship was friendly and solid. We were friends outside of our official roles and spent a lot of time joking around. At this scene, Naomi had to wear her game face. Every captain and chief in the county was running around and any public information procedures would be handled by the book. Sheriff deputies blocked all hotel entrances.

By 1:45 a.m., the injured had been removed, most of

the other partiers had gone home, and the parking lot was three-quarters empty. For the previous thirty minutes, I had waited with two newspaper reporters for the opportunity to look inside. Naomi was doing her best to accommodate us, but I didn't realize it. At about 2:15 a.m., after wandering around and not being able to find her for another thirty minutes, I left. I found out the next day that ten minutes after I departed, they opened the doors.

I missed blood, I missed torn curtains, I missed shrapnel holes in the ceiling, and I missed a mess. Naomi teased me about it for months.

"You could have been inside. Inside! You blew it," she'd remind.

Meanwhile, after the short drive home, I was obligated to call our assignment editor, Jim Vangrove. Despite the wee hour, it was mandatory that I wake him up and report the situation. He gave me the low-down on what was expected and what steps to take the next day. He was very appreciative of my efforts and very excited about the exclusive. He wanted me to edit an extra version of the piece for the CBS network feed and for CNN and FNN (Florida News Network).

The next morning, I figured out a way to play golf *and* get everything accomplished. For the next few days after that, I'd rationalize my blown opportunity.

I already had more than enough video than I knew what to do with, great sound bites, and cool shots and sounds, I thought. *The blood would have been sensory overload. I had already written the next day's story in the parking lot, I had to play golf in the morning, and I had an exclusive story and a half day to edit it*, a portion of my brain argued. *I was busting my ass on this job, and they were paying me only fifteen grand a year!*

Okay, so that was all bullshit. In reality, missing the indoor scenes pissed me off. Blowing the chance for the "icing on the cake" was a disappointment. Even if I didn't use the blood scenes the next day, the door would have been open for an automatic and very effective follow-up story.

Fortunately, two weeks later, I landed a follow-up anyway — another exclusive: an interview with victim Scott Jones in his Port Charlotte home. Well known among his peers for his upbeat attitude, Scott managed to keep his positive outlook despite the personal tragedy of losing his leg. His family prayed for strength and gave thanks, as Scott very easily could have been killed. His story became one I'd never forget, one that always reminded me how fragile life is and how easily danger can lurk unexpectedly.

Of course, in Florida, "unexpected" often also means "bizarre."

While moving to Fort Myers in August 1990, driving south, towing a U-Haul trailer, I'll never forget passing two women whose car had apparently broken down by the side of the road. They were pulled off just short of an overpass. I slowed to look. They were both out of the car, and a man had stopped a few car lengths behind to help them. The image of the women, especially the tall blonde, stuck in my mind. I got a decent look at her face and hair. The second gal was shorter with dark hair.

Usually when a *wow* moment occurs, we recognize a celebrity or someone or something from our past. With these women, the *wow* moment actually came months later, after serial killer Aileen Wuornos and her companion, Tyria Moore, had been caught. I flashed back to those few moments on Interstate 75.

Oh my God, I remembered, *that was them.*

Had I contemplated stopping to help them? I might have; I'd help damsels in distress on the side of a highway. But the other guy had already stopped to help. What happened to him? Did he become a murder victim?

After killing at least seven men, Wuornos was executed via lethal injection in 2002. Numerous films and books have documented her killing spree. Charlize Theron won an Oscar for portraying Wuornos in the movie *Monster* released in 2003.

I'm pretty darn sure it was her and Moore by the side of the road: a monster in the swamp; an appropriate welcome for any news reporter moving to the Sunshine State.

Fort Myers was a very competitive stepping-stone TV market at the time for some eventual big time talent. Hoda Kotb of Today Show *fame was one of our news reporters and a weekend anchor at WINK. Shepard Smith of* FOX News *was a reporter and anchor at our main competitor WBBH-TV at the time. Many others left southeast Florida for big markets like Philadelphia, Cleveland, Boston, and New York. They worked our asses off frankly, and weeded out those less talented and determined.*

YouTube clip: Simmer WINK-TV Man

> "I was going in total slow motion the whole entire time, looking around the valley, thinking, *God, what a beautiful place this is, and gee, you know, how odd . . .* I was just absolutely sure my life was over. So strange. I'd say it was a peak experience."

> **Former hostage Peter O'Callaghan, September 1995**

THE HOSTAGE

On Wednesday, August 5, 1992, photographer Peter O'Callaghan and I started the day slowly. Not much was happening on another weak news day at KGMB-TV in Hawaii. It was about eleven a.m. when our assignment manager, Brenda Salgado, also known fondly as Brendude, although she was anything but, roused us from a conversation in one of the edit bays.

A manhunt: a known criminal had jumped parole. Apparently considered armed and dangerous, Ulysses Kim was playing hide-and-seek with the sheriff's department in a neighbourhood near the Punchbowl Crater in

Honolulu. Peter and I were assigned to join the deputies from the State of Hawaii in their search, get the details on Kim's background, and shoot video of the areas he had been seen.

Our shooting and interviewing duties were done in an hour. The rest of the afternoon we simply sat and waited. We watched deputies and dogs search and sniff for clues. We ran around town chasing a few leads, but they all turned out to be rumours about Kim's whereabouts. The fugitive never turned up.

Peter and I headed back to the station to put together stories for the five and six p.m. newscasts. At dusk, the deputies postponed their search. As usual, I wrapped up my work, prepped for the next day, and, on this occasion, headed home to get ready for a softball game. Another day, another half dollar.

My evening turned out to be more frustrating than my afternoon. I went an inexcusable oh-for-three in my at-bats. To make matters worse, during my second time at the plate, I seemed to rip a muscle in my lower back. Our team of local writers and advertising men lost.

The next morning, I had a hard time standing up. The back pain, combined with an unexpected head cold, left me temporarily bedridden and angry. Until this point, I hadn't ever missed a day of work due to injury or sickness. I called in.

"Bren-dude, I'm done," I stated. "I'm illin' and I tore my back up last night. Sorry."

The Kim situation never crossed my mind. Later, I'd hear the remarkable tale of how the day unfolded. I had figuratively, and almost literally, dodged a potential bullet.

In my absence, Peter was hooked up with college intern, Tiffany Spencer. Tiffany had spent the summer attempting to learn as much as possible about the reporting business. August 6, 1992, became the ultimate initiation day.

The Ulysses Kim search had picked up at dawn where it had left off the evening before. Peter began the day alone, sitting in the news van listening to the police scanner, close to their command post. Peter and the cops were positioned about a third of the way up Tantalus, a lush neighbourhood above and behind Punchbowl in Honolulu. Looking from the ocean, Tantalus sits above an area called Makiki. Manoa Valley stretches back below to the right; Pauoa Valley to the left. The Ko'olau Range rises above it all, separating Honolulu from Kailua and the windward side of Oahu. Two roads meet at the top of Tantalus. Tantalus Drive begins at its base near Pauoa to the left; Round Top Drive starts from the Manoa side.

"I'm writing down on a piece of paper where the guy's gone," Peter remembers. "He had his breakfast at this little old lady's, Mrs. Akana. And I got the address because she called it in after he left because she thought he was kind of suspicious. He supposedly spent the night at some chick's house down at the back of this road where the cop command centre was. The mother had seen him, he had shown 'em the gun, and they called it in. So he'd been spotted all over the place."

Ninety minutes after Peter arrived on the scene, Brenda drove a news van over and dropped off Tiffany.

"Here's Tiffany, who's, like, this intern, right," Peter explains. "Brenda says [Tiffany] doesn't have anything to do, she's gonna do a package [news piece] on whatever you guys come up with. Just sit here and listen, and that's basically what we did."

What a team. Peter O'Callaghan and Tiffany Spencer represented complete opposites. Describing Peter as flamboyant was an understatement. He could be loud, he could be obnoxious, and he was almost always a joy to work with. A full-blooded Irishman from Chicago who grew up in the age of psychedelics, Pete enjoyed being the centre of attention. His outgoing and generally irreverent nature made a social occasion out of work, rest, or play. At the same time, he enjoyed his life as a family man, living on the lush windward side of Oahu with his wife and young daughter. Big, bulky, and blond, Peter's zest for life flickered in his spirited blue eyes.

Tiffany was a relative unknown. Tall, buxom, Mormon, and married: that summed up the newsroom's general knowledge of this Brigham Young University coed. She made up for her naïvete and lack of experience with a sometimes fiery perseverance.

On this particular assignment, she'd show a "go get 'em" attitude that the normally uninspired news staff lacked.

On Wednesday, we had learned that Kim was carrying a scanner of his own. He knew where most of the police units were located. On Thursday, the police tried to use this knowledge to their advantage.

"They said they were calling off the search," Tiffany recalls. "They were hoping Ulysses Kim would come out of hiding. But they were not *actually* calling off the search. We figured that out, so we started going door to door around the neighbourhood asking, 'Did you see Ulysses Kim? Was he here?'"

The two decided to visit the elderly woman who reported getting a visit from the fugitive during breakfast. On the way down Mrs. Akana's driveway, the two shared an amazing conversation. The ultimate foreshadowing.

"I'm telling you, I think this was psychic," Peter recalls. "When we're walking down there, I go, 'Now lookit, if anyone gets held hostage, it's gonna be you because I'm a father.' And she goes, 'Oh no, no, it couldn't be me, my husband would miss me way too much.' Can you believe that?

"I had really kind of forgotten saying it," Peter remembered, "but Tiffany reminded me, and I knew exactly what I had said, it was just, like, crystal clear. It's really weird."

Mrs. Akana told Peter and Tiffany everything they wanted to hear, only she wouldn't do it on camera.

It's relatively common to arrive at a scene and have a witness or participant in a story not want to talk to the cameras. This is especially true in Hawaii because of the traditional Asian values. Visiting Japanese women, or locals of Japanese descent, particularly the older ones, could be most difficult. It's not their place to speak to a stranger carrying a camera. Some Japanese women visiting the beach will actually scurry and hide when they see someone shooting video.

A reporter can sneak an interview, or they can try to persuade a person to talk. It's not uncommon to see a reporter begging, depending on the importance and timing of the story. Persuasion is the only option once you lose the element of surprise. If the person won't budge, then make the best of it. Often after asking once, chit-chatting for a while, and then asking again, an interviewer will get the go-ahead.

In Mrs. Akana's case, she wasn't budging. Her husband had died recently, so she didn't have his advice or support. Luckily for Tiffany and Peter, she had no problem with telling the whole story off-camera. At least they'd get every detail.

"She proceeded to tell me the entire incident — how he came in, he didn't threaten her, he just asked her if he could use the phone," Tiffany remembers. "Then she showed us how he left her home through the backyard and went into the valley, because it was lush and thick and it was a great place for him to hide."

The twosome decided to move on, to find other locations in the area to check for leads. After thanking Mrs. Akana and heading up the driveway with Tiffany, Peter spotted the crew from Channel 4. Reporter Keoki Kerr and photographer Bob Guanzon were making their way toward Akana's house.

"Keoki and Bob were headed down to the house, so we decided to head right back down with them," Tiffany says.

Rarely does a reporter let a rival determine his or her next move, especially if it means backtracking. In this case, however, Peter and Tiffany had some unfinished business they could handle. Tiffany could do an on-camera stand-up at the scene. Plus, the news biz was pretty casual in Alohaland, and the group could catch up and "talk story."

Their decision to backtrack was monumental.

Tiffany and Peter decided to set up near the bushes at the rear edge of the yard. The valley dropped off dramatically just behind the thick brush. Approximately twenty-five feet separated the house from the edge of the valley. A couple of steps led up to a small porch and back door on the rear of the home.

"We were all in the backyard. We all heard a rustling," Tiffany describes, "and Ulysses Kim just popped up out of the bushes. It looked like he just hopped up out of nowhere. He just stood there in a daze, and it was obvious he was on something. He just kind of . . . nobody said anything, then he looked at us and asked if we were with the news. We said yes."

For Peter, the next thirty minutes would unravel in slow motion.

"Now [Mrs. Akana] is on the back porch," Peter starts. "It's Keoki, Tiffany, Bob, and myself, right? I'm talking to the lady on the [porch], and here comes the guy, walking up the steep cliff. We couldn't believe it. He's got a coat over his [right] hand here, and he had a scanner in his other hand. I start picking up the camera, I figure he's going to give himself up. I figure he's tired and realizes they're gonna kill him and all this other stuff.

"He goes, 'No no, we'll have none of that.' He's got this dopey look on his face and waves, 'Put the camera back down.' Then I look at Bob and I go, 'That's the guy?' and he goes, 'Yeah, that's the guy.'

"Mrs. Akana is standing right there on the back porch of her place there, and he's looking at her going, 'Uuuuuuuhhhhhh.' So I turn and start to push her into her house, and I'm, like, 'Go hide, go hide, go anywhere to hide.' He walks right up to [Tiffany and Keoki], and I'm with this lady going, 'Hey, you should get out of here.' I push her in her house."

For Tiffany, the next few moments were a blur.

"The next thing I remember," she recalls, "I turned around, and Ulysses Kim has the gun to Peter's back, and he's ordering him into the house. Peter yells back and says, 'Get outta here!'"

"I can't figure out why he chose me, that's what really blows me away," Peter wonders aloud. "Because Keoki Kerr, obviously on television . . . probably because I moved, or probably because I had put the camera up in the beginning.

"Anyway, I push this woman into the house and turn around to look at what's going on, and he was right there. The jacket was down and he had a shotgun and he dug it right into my side. He just came straight across . . . he ran across the yard and came right up behind me. I had my back turned for a second; when I turned back around there he was.

"I'm, like, 'Fuck, oh no, no, no, you've got to be mistaken, I can't . . . I can't do anything.' He says, 'No, shut up, you're going to take me outta here. You're gonna get me out of this valley.' I'm, like, 'I can't get you out of this valley, I can't do anything, I da . . . da . . . da . . . ahhhh . . . whatever.' He goes, 'Shut the fuck up, or I'm gonna blow your head off.'"

Mrs. Akana watched this exchange and then retreated into a bedroom. Kim backed Peter into the house. Tiffany ran and hid around the side of the house with Keoki and called 911 on her cell phone (actually, KGMB's cell phone; personal cell phones were uncommon at this point). Channel 4 photographer Guanzon dropped his equipment, ran around the side of the house, quickly scaled a ten-foot stone wall, and ran to get police.

Peter's life was in the hands of a stoned fugitive. We learned later that Kim was apparently on an "ice" (crystal methamphetamine) buzz that lasted for more than 140 hours.

Kim led Peter through the house, had him unlock the front door, and began backing him up an outdoor stairway. By now the police radios were jamming with information on the hostage situation.

"He had the gun in my gut and wants me to walk him up these stairs and up to where there are cops everywhere," recalls Peter. "These cops — who had been acting like they were all going away — all the SWAT guys, sixty of them coming down from the top, sixty of them coming up from the bottom, all with their SWAT jackets on and their shotguns and all this shit. I mean, it's like cops everywhere. I mean *everywhere*.

"He's facing me, walking me up the stairs backwards, and he goes, 'Put the camera down.' So I put the camera down. He turns me around and puts the gun up my back and marches me up there. He walks me up to Channel 4's car and says, 'Don't look at those cops, just walk over to this news car, get in, and drive away.' I'm trying to explain to him it's Channel 4's news car. I don't have the keys, I can't drive it, I don't have them. He goes, 'Try the doors!' He's getting really . . . he's obviously out of his mind.'"

Peter's own news van was parked a quarter-mile away. Fortunate, because Kim would have no opportunity to ride off with Peter; unfortunate, because this development left Kim angry, with very few alternatives.

Whether Peter lived or died would be determined in the next few moments.

Peter continued to try all of the doors while Kim yelled warnings to police.

"He's yelling at them, 'Get the keys to this car! Get the keys to this fucking car or I'm going to waste this *haole*!'" The two stayed close together near the car as Kim continued to yell threats for another minute.

"Finally he says, 'Kneel down.' And I'm, like, 'Ahh, c'mon man, I didn't do anything to you.' He goes, 'Kneel down!'" Peter went to his knees as Kim centred the shotgun on his back.

"He's standing there, yelling, 'You know, I'm fucking serious, I'm gonna kill this *haole* motherfucker if you don't get the keys to this car!' Then he tells me to lie down on my face."

At this point, Peter believed his life was over.

"I wasn't really into going down on my face. He pushes me down and has the gun right here, pushed up against the back of my head. The *back* of my head.

"He goes, 'If you fuckers think you can take me down, take your best shot because I'm gonna waste this guy or get out of this valley.'"

The sound of a gunshot echoed.

"Some cop . . . shot him. Shot him in the neck."

Peter heard the shot, panicked briefly, but then saw the shotgun drop. It fell ten inches from his face and bounced. It was pointed directly at his head.

Peter was almost killed by a fugitive and then almost shot by accident. That's when adrenaline took over.

"The gun is there and all I'm thinking about is the gun. I rolled over and grabbed the gun in one motion. I'm standing there over the guy, going, 'You fucker, how do you like this, you fucking . . . ' If you listen to the [news] tape, I'm just beside myself."

Photographers from the two other local TV news stations had arrived in time to shoot a portion of the crisis. Tiffany and Keoki heard the shot and ran up the hill. The police converged on Peter.

"They're all yelling at once, 'Put the gun down, put the gun down!' I'm just gone, you know what I'm saying. I'm not thinking of anything except I'm gonna get this guy.

"Then this one cop goes, 'C'mon, please put the gun down, it's hot out here . . . c'mon, let's just all go home, put the gun down.' I mean, just like that. I mean, everyone else is yelling at the top of their voices . . . some cop is saying . . . treating me like . . . *please* put the gun down, ha, ha, ha.

"This is a time when my daughter is, like, two years old, and it's weird, what's going through my head, 'Well, he did say please.' So I dropped the gun, ran, and got the camera, and started shooting."

Peter thought Kim was dead. He was bleeding from the neck and lying motionless on his stomach.

"It was really ugly," Peter continues. "I'm shooting this whole thing and the cops are telling me to get out of there. Cops are moving us back, literally a guy with a dog is pushing me with his hands to back away from there. So I'm like, 'Fine, let's get the hell out of here, I've had it with this.'"

Peter and Tiffany prepared to leave but couldn't. The police realized they needed to detain Peter for questioning. At the same time, KGMB photographer Terry Hunter arrived.

"I hiked up to a side street where I was surprised to see a SWAT team and a huge bus," Terry describes. "Lots of cops, I mean, it was an army of law enforcement people up there. And Peter was there. I was delighted to see he was okay, and he told me what happened. Then he tried to give me the tape from his camera."

That's when the hostage drama became a first-amendment crisis. Peter had rolled tape and recorded video on his camera before being taken hostage and then again right after dropping the gun. He knew he would be tied up with questioning for a while, so he handed Terry the tape.

"Immediately, six HPD guys are on me, telling me I can't take the tape because it's evidence. I told them it was our tape and we needed to have it, that we'd be happy to make a copy. It was late in the afternoon, and we needed to get it on the newscast.

"They would have none of it," Terry adds. "They actually grabbed me and took the tape from me. They said it was evidence."

Terry wasn't about to overwhelm a cop, let alone a herd of them. In his midforties, standing about five-foot-nine and slight, Terry's a former English professor turned movie critic, reminiscent of a protestant Woody Allen.

"I realized then that if I had any hope of getting that tape, I had to be super nice. So I changed my tone and said, 'Look, is there some way we can get a copy?'"

"The guy in charge of the SWAT team said it was okay to turn over the tape," Peter points out. "He wanted to make sure I hadn't rolled the whole time [while captive], which I hadn't. I wish I had but I was unable to. The camera I used that day was too noisy turning on and off and Kim would have heard it clicking. It was the cop in charge of the scene by the command centre who saw me give the tape to Terry and took it out of his pocket."

Terry's point of contention was that Channel 2 and Channel 4 had been rolling and police weren't confiscating those tapes. Why should Channel 9 give up its copy?

"Finally they agreed," says Terry. "A cop and I went with the tape to the station. We made a dub of the tape, they gave the copy to us and took the original. Later on, we filed complaints and all that with the police department but it didn't do any good. They had basically done something illegal and they got away with it, as they tend to do in situations like that."

As Terry negotiated, Tiffany Spencer had returned to the station to do some urgent lobbying of her own.

"[Managing Editor and anchor] Bob Jones told me that they were going to give the story to [police reporter] Jerry Drelling, which was a logical assumption because I was only an intern," Tiffany remembers. "But I fought for the story. I told Bob Jones I was going to do the story, it was my story, and he agreed. I did the story and afterwards Bob came and said that I had shown him I had guts, and that when my internship was over he'd offer me a part-time job. He didn't have a full-time job at that point."

A little more than a week later, Tiffany was working part-time. Two weeks later, reporter Collette Pritchard left permanently for the mainland and Tiffany was hired full-time. A break is only a break if the opportunity is fulfilled.

"My chances of getting a job here permanently were very slim, but because of that incident, I got hired."

Peter returned to the station in time for the five o'clock news. Both he and Terry joined the anchors on the set to describe the details of the afternoon on live television.

"Me on set, which was totally ridiculous," Peter recalls. "I mean, I was totally a mess, dressed like a pig, sweating, and just looked horrible."

Not to mention the trauma. Despite that, and not unexpectedly for those who worked at KGMB, the management thought of the station first.

"Our camera supervisor comes back and goes, 'How are ya, are ya okay?' He goes, 'You know, I can't spare you tomorrow, you're gonna have to come in,'" Peter recalls. "I was, like, 'Fine, whatever.' I was just totally in shock."

Bob Jones came back and told Peter that no matter what anyone said, Peter was not coming to work the next day. Terry was also flabbergasted.

"What happened to Peter was such a shocking thing, I mean, he really thought he was going to die," Terry states. "That's major trauma, that's like being in Vietnam for an afternoon you know? And . . . I had to help talk the station into giving Peter the next day off. They were just gonna let him go to work like nothing happened. And that just appalled me, it really did."

Peter put the work request in perspective.

"I probably should have gone to work because the next morning everybody on the fucking planet was calling me."

Peter would eventually appear on the *Oprah* show, on an episode about news people who became the news. It seemed to be an exciting conclusion to the saga for Peter's friends and well-wishers. For Peter himself, the notoriety

The view of Waikiki Beach in the foreground and downtown Honolulu in the distance from the top of the Diamond Head crater. Peter was taken hostage in the foothills off to the right.

was fleeting. But the emotional impact of the trauma will last.

"Pretty much a peak experience," Peter reflects. "I think I learned a couple of things. First of all, death is so easy, man. You could just be gone like that. In an instant, and it's not scary and it's not bad. I think what's really weird is the idea of dying . . . the death. Death seems like it's just *ahhhh*, it's the dying that seems like it could be a real drag."

"I can't even imagine going through what he went through," Terry adds. "I think everybody noticed that Peter was upset for a long, long, long time after that. I mean, he was just louder, and more amped . . . and he had to deal with the guy saying [in court] that when he finally got out of jail he was going to come after Peter."

"It fucked me up for a while," Peter concludes.

———————————

Ulysses Kim served time in the Halawa Correctional Facility and on the mainland due to overcrowding in Hawaii. He won a $199,000 settlement in 1999 for apparent mistreatment at Halawa. He was arrested again in 2007 not long after his release and again in 2012 and 2013 for various offenses.

Peter and his family moved to the mainland three years after the incident.

Tiffany is a leading real estate agent on the island of Kauai where she lives with her husband and kids.

Terry and his wife live on Oahu. Besides being a photog', he's been the preeminent movie reviewer on the local TV news since the early 1990s.

> "We might be experiencing
> some lumpy air today."

**Continental Airlines captain before
Honolulu to Sydney, November 1988**

FLIGHTS

On a Horizon Air flight from Boise, Idaho, to Portland, Oregon, in 1998, the flight attendant in the front of the plane was yelling to the one in the back, "Get down, get down!" The aircraft appeared to be plummeting through turbulence. We weren't enjoying ourselves. That was my 420th flight.

On a flight from Honolulu to L.A. in June 1995, my 215th, the jumbo jet we were in was about to land. About 300 feet or so off the ground, the engines fired back up to full throttle, the wheels came up, and the beast headed back out over the Pacific.

"There was a plane on the runway," the pilot informed us. "We're gonna come around and try that again." My heart was pumping and my palms were sweating for the ten- or twelve-minute reapproach that seemed to take about an hour.

On a Porter Airlines flight in March 2013 to little Billy Bishop Airport (also known as the Island Airport because it's built on an island in Lake Ontario, just off downtown Toronto), my 1,208th flight, we were only about 100 feet from the ground when the wheels came back up.

"We'll come around and try that again," the pilot finished after explaining that we were moving too quickly to attempt a landing. Seemed better than bouncing into Lake Ontario. Not that big a deal, but it did get my heart pumping again.

I'm not the most organized cat in the world, nor am I the anal-retentive type, but for whatever reason, starting just a few flights into my long travel career, I decided to log them. On pieces of cardboard, usually the backs of reporters' notebooks, I write in rows the month and year, the airline, the departure city, draw an arrow, and the arrival city. Often there are extra cities and arrows in between to mark the legs of each journey. I didn't count my two skydives. The plane has to take off *and* land with me in it to count as a flight. Let's hope that trend continues.

On my 29th flight, from Honolulu to Sydney, Australia, in December 1988, our airplane hit an air-pocket over the equatorial doldrums. We dropped a few thousand feet. My buddy Tom Towers and I were playing cards; in fact, I was whipping him for about the eleventh time out of twelve at a French-Canadian game called Mille Bornes. Suddenly, our jumbo jet started falling. Our stomachs rose to our throats, only to fall back down into place with gusto as the plane sank into some solid air. At the beginning of that flight, the pilot had warned us about moderate turbulence. He gave no warning about the plane dropping like a rock near the equator, where the cyclogenesis that creates weather systems in the northern and southern hemispheres is practically non-existent. There's no warning to give.

The term "being in the doldrums" came from that area of the sea, where sailing vessels in olden days would get stranded in open water for days due to lack of wind. In modern times, at 33,000 feet above that calm, open water, the lack of high-pressure systems and such leaves a little more space for those aforementioned air pockets.

Twice I was on Aloha Island Air flights between Honolulu and Lanai, and it felt like some little-kid-God had our airplane on a rubber band, bouncing us up and down between the islands. On one of those occasions, the only passengers on the flight were my then-wife, Nora, me, and our friend Sweetie Nelson. It was December 1993, my 155th.

As bad and as terrifying as some of these experiences in the air were, the two worst-ever flights were the 52nd and 400th.

The former was a Midway Airlines flight between Chicago and Detroit in July 1990. Northwest, the airline I was originally scheduled to fly, cancelled all of its evening flights due to thunderstorms. Midway was, like, "Hell yes, we're going!" I paid fifty bucks to hop on this alternative. I was heading to a party to meet a bunch of college friends and wasn't about to miss it.

It. Was. A. Live. Ing. Night. Mare.

We took off, hit the clouds, and bounced violently through the sky for the next forty-five minutes. The lady next to me worked for the Internal Revenue Service, was doing paperwork, and never batted an eye. I figured she was either as cool as a cucumber or, because she worked for the IRS, she didn't give a shit whether we crashed.

We lurched, we plunged, we climbed, we thumped, and we rattled continuously. The wings actually seemed to flap as I gripped the armrests with my fingers and the floor with my toes, through my shoes. When we came down out of the clouds near Detroit, the transition to the smooth air was stark. What a great feeling of relief that was, although I think the journey took about four years off my life.

Flight 400 was a Delta flight with the Idaho Steelheads hockey team between Fresno, California, and Reno, Nevada, in March 1998. We were going from a game against the Fighting Falcons to a game against the Renegades, a team coached by Ron "Flockey Hockey" Flockhart. Flockhart had been suspended for a game or two for going nuts on a ref, so during the match he sat next to us in the press box and drank beer. The flight there was so bad, I thought Steelheads captain, Jamie Cooke, had suffered a heart attack. He turned blue, frozen, and speechless. I recall a lot of lateral movement, like the plane was being blown sideways, and then we'd just drop for a second or two before climbing back up.

This was life in the old WCHL. The West Coast Hockey League, known to many as the "Western Cocktail Holiday League," was the only AA circuit where all of the teams flew everywhere, instead of travelling by bus, except for between Fresno and Bakersfield, California. For that reason, and a respectably high weekly salary cap, the league attracted some decent former NHLers and AHLers. Ex–Philadelphia Flyer and L.A. King (and Gretzky's childhood chum) Len Hachborn played for the San Diego Gulls; ex–Washington Capital and Detroit Red Wing Darren Veitch played for Phoenix; ex–Ottawa Senator Darcy Loewen played for Idaho; and there were many others.

Most flights were on Southwest Airlines with its cattle-call boarding process. It was open, every-man-for-himself seating. Southwest used to have 737s with two areas, one in the middle of the plane and one in the back, where three seats faced three seats across from one another on both sides of the aisle. It was funky sitting backwards for take-off and landing, but the "lounge" made for easy and entertaining card playing. Six or seven of us would sit together in the lounges and play Snarples literally from the time we sat down until the plane pulled up to the destination gate. The "ding" of the captain parking the plane and turning off the seat belt sign marked the official end of the game.

On yet another Southwest flight, in December 1999, while many of the other passengers moaned and gasped and gripped as we tried and failed three times to descend through a thick fog into Seattle, our little card playing group hardly noticed the drama at all, simply relishing the fact that we got to squeeze in another hand or two.

Oddly, the 300th and 500th flights were also significant. Life lined up so that these big, round numbers always seemed to match significant, benchmark flights.

Flight 100 came in Hawaii in September 1992 during

my days as a news reporter at KGMB-TV. We left Kahului Airport on Maui on a little Twin Piper propeller plane, what I referred to as a "Chevette with wings." (The Chevrolet Chevette was a little smaller than a Honda Civic is now.) The proprietor and pilot of All Pacific Air was hired by the station to fly me and a camera guy around the perimeter of Haleakala (Holl-lay-ock-a-la) in search of the remains of a tour helicopter that had crashed. On a fixed-wing, four-seat aircraft, ripping through the trade winds, we bounced along the side of a 10,000-foot-high mountain, hoping to spot carnage. The Australian-born chopper pilot and the six Japanese tourists on board were dead. That we knew. We just didn't know where to find them.

Haleakala in English means the "house of the sun." It's the giant, dormant volcano that makes up the eastern half of the island, and about 75 percent of Maui's land area in general. Not sure what dormant means; I guess it means "barely not active," since Haleakala has erupted with lava flow three times in the last 900 years, the last time less than 300 years ago.

Sitting in the back seat with my knees in my face, I wasn't worried about being swallowed up by lava, but I was worried about All Pacific returning safely to the airport. There was cloud cover from the summit down to about 7,000 feet, preventing us from seeing the top of the mountain, but not from seeing the blue-coloured wreckage. What did prevent us from spotting successfully was the fact the chopper had crashed into a gulch at about the 3,000-foot mark. It was spotted later and photographed from another helicopter.

I do recall interviewing the pilot's daughter. She was

a hottie, and I barely managed to resist the temptation to hit on her. Dictionary definition of "too soon," I guess.

She was pretty calm and pragmatic about the whole thing. Her now-late father, Peter Middleton, had been buzzing around the islands for two decades, and she was well aware of the risks. We also had to interview the tour-company people from Hawaii Helicopters. It was one of those moments when you couldn't help but feel like an asshole, asking about recently killed people and the safety record of the business. I didn't enjoy the vulture element to local news.

Much like the two dozen flights before and after my 100th, the two dozen or so before and after my 200th flight were also very routine; Honolulu to Hilo, to Kahului, or to Lahui and back, or a trip to the mainland to visit friends and family. The somewhat-monumental flight 200 came as the Hawaii portion of my career wound down. I was in New York, staying with a bunch of goons, college and post-college buddies, looking to interview for gigs and relocate, when we randomly decided to go to Jamaica.

It was January 1995, and we flew Air Jamaica. We paid a whopping twenty-five dollars to upgrade to first class and drink champagne and enjoy extra legroom. We got it simply by asking at check-in. All but one of the six of us moved up. It was remarkably casual, but then again, we *were* flying to the land of the Rastafarians.

This was my first trip to the Caribbean. It's incredibly undeveloped in a lot of ways — sorry, "developing"— a fact that hit us in the face as we rode by endless tin shanties along the side of the road on the way from the airport at Montego Bay to Negril. The general population is extremely poor, and the town was considered a bit sketchy. This didn't prevent us from roaming out into the local scene and attending reggae concerts. We also frog-manned into Hedonism II.

We weren't staying at the all-inclusive luxury resort; we were staying next to it. Pointe Village featured standard condo rentals, a pool, and some evening entertainment on the beach. There were families.

At Hedonism, there weren't families. There were nude heterosexuals playing shuffleboard, doing naughty things in the hot tubs, and swinging on a beach trapeze. The beach was sort of cut in half and there was a clothed side as well, but those wearing bikinis or shorts weren't allowed to cross the line into "Nude World" unless they dropped their skivvies.

Our fearless leader Tommy, who had arranged our accommodations and proximity to Hedonism, wanted us to experience the resort's famous weekly toga party one evening.

We did this by going Navy Seal.

One by one we frog-manned from Point Village to Hedonism. There were guards at the fences that ran down between the properties to the beach, so we had to take the water route. In the dark, one guy would slowly side paddle or backstroke out about sixty yards, turn left, slowly paddle another 100 yards beyond the swim ropes that marked Hedonism's area, and then turn and quietly make his way under that rope to the shore. This would be a beach landing the exact opposite of Normandy. There were no snipers; the only bombshells were inside. Every two minutes or so, another one of us would arrive. Really good toga party. I met two sisters from St. Louis, and I don't mean nuns.

The strange coincidence with significant flights continued with flight 300. It was on Delta, flying back from my one and only Super Bowl. Brett Favre had led the Green Bay Packers to a 35–21 victory over Drew Bledsoe's Patriots at Super Bowl XXXI in New Orleans in 1997. Among a number of tantalizing special teams runs, Former Michigan Wolverine, Desmond Howard, had a ninety-nine-yard kickoff return for a touchdown and was named MVP. New Orleans makes Las Vegas look like church; plus, it is authentic debauchery, not commercialized or somewhat fabricated.

The best part about the trip was that Albertson's grocery stores, headquartered in Boise, Idaho, paid for the whole thing, with some help from the local Pepsi distributor. The late Jim Reynolds, an Albertson's VP at the time, loved our local sports radio station and was a huge supporter of the new hockey team, the Idaho Steelheads, who were one winter away from their inaugural season. I was to be their play-by-play man and was already handling the same gig in the summer for the local baseball team, the Boise Hawks of the short-season, A-ball Northwest League. Both clubs were owned by a group of men who called themselves Diamond Sports, as innovative and progressive an organization as you could find in minor-league business. I hosted an hour-long talk show in the off-seasons called *Pepsi Proline*. Standard stuff, we took calls from local fans and interviewed guests by phone, many of them from the NHL level. We were trying to entertain, educate, and inundate our inexperienced hockey audience, who were also our potential season-ticket buyers.

During my first winter in Boise, while there was yet to be a hockey team, Jim agreed to the wonderful idea of sending me and a sidekick to the Super Bowl.

"What the hell, let's do it," he said.

He gave us two corporate tickets to the game and also paid for our flights and accommodations. "Our" included local celebrity golf pro, Thor Swensson, and myself. "The Mighty" Thor had Boise's only golf simulator at the time, was a regular on a local sports talk show, and had a larger-than-life persona. He was allegedly qualified to be my "radio producer" because of his creative organizational skills. Thor had previously invited Jack Daniels to my already-out-of-hand thirty-second birthday party. What better guy to bring to the Super Bowl?

Reporting from New Orleans during Super Bowl week was the only time I ever drank before going on the air, and I did it on purpose, because the show was entirely on tape. We weren't there on press credentials and we weren't interviewing football players; we were there to report on the scene and the atmosphere. Our show ran Monday through Friday for an hour at six p.m. mountain time. During Super Bowl Week, we'd head onto the very crowded streets each night at about eleven p.m., with a tape recorder, a couple of hurricanes in us and another in hand. We'd walk into bars and interview Packers fans and Patriots fans and anyone resembling a celebrity. Naturally, we included the hottest women we could possibly find to talk football. Thor, an extraordinary production assistant, held my drink while I held the microphone and actually gathered material. As for celebs, they were all sports types if I remember: Dan Patrick from ESPN, former NFL coach Jerry Glanville, and Pat O'Brien from CBS among them.

At about midnight, we'd wrap up with about forty minutes of material, drop the recorder off in the room, and proceed back outside for a night of revelry. The next evening before heading out to duplicate the assignment, we'd host the live portion of the radio program. We'd set up the remote equipment in the hotel room, basically a mixer box with two headsets connected via phone line to the studio back home — we'd welcome everyone to the show, shoot the shit for a bit, and then hit Play on the tape recorder. Forty minutes later, having stopped it a couple of times for commercial breaks, we'd hit stop for good, chat live about any football news, and then say goodbye.

Repeat effort five times, then have Saturday off, and then go to the Super Bowl on Sunday.

Mr. Reynolds was also responsible for me and my wife Nora attending the Fiesta Bowl in Tempe, Arizona, in 1999, when the Tennessee Volunteers defeated the Florida State Seminoles for college football's national championship. It was the game in which Vol's quarterback Tee Martin threw a seventy-nine-yard touchdown bomb to Peerless Price in the fourth quarter to put the game away. That's all I really remember, other than the FSU band playing the Tomahawk chop-chop theme and the Tennessee band playing "Rocky Top" incessantly. Beyond incessantly. Like, I'm going to shoot all of you geeks if you don't stop, incessantly.

Thank you, Jim Reynolds. Regardless of the gifts of those two great junkets, he was indeed a great, great guy and a loving father. Rest in peace.

Fatherhood would actually be the theme for flight number 500. Like a dream — a spontaneous flight home to witness the birth of my son in June 1999.

Of course, Mom couldn't dilate *before* I got on the ten-hour overnight bus trip to Medford, Oregon, for the start of a five-game series between the Boise Hawks and the Southern Oregon Timberjacks. She instead reached the point of no return five minutes after my head hit the pillow for the morning nap that ensued immediately after I got there. Up, to the Medford airport, Horizon Air to Portland, and then to Boise.

A few hours later, I popped home from the hospital to take our Rottweiler out for a walk. Just after I got there, a doctor declared Mom ready to pop. I rushed back for a middle-of-the-night umbilical cord cut. My son fit into the palms of my two hands.

The fact that this momentous event coincided with my 500th flight is uncanny, but that's where the wicked-cool pattern stopped — until flight 1,000.

Just for shits and giggles: flight 600 was Seattle to Anchorage on Alaska Airlines in November 2000; 700 was Detroit to Chicago on Southwest in 2002; 800 was Chicago to Philadelphia in December 2004; and number 900 was Boston to Ottawa in March 2006 on the Boston Bruins team charter. Nothing occurred out of the ordinary.

The monumental 1,000th career flight came during a trip to Africa to film a documentary with Right To Play. In June 2007, Bruins defenceman Andrew Ference, Florida Panthers D-man Steve "Monty" Montador, Mark

Steve Montador, Mark Brender, Andrew Ference, and me, all hopping on my 1,000th flight.

Brender of Right To Play, videographer Pat Gamere from New England Sports Network, and I all flew a domestic flight on Air Tanzania from Dar es Salaam, the big city on the coast, to Mwanza, the biggest city on Lake Victoria. Four of us stood in a line right next to the stairs of the airplane while Gamere took our picture. Monty held up a single index finger while the rest of us stood next to him and held up zeros. Brender screwed it up a bit; Andrew and I made zeros by making a little circle with our hands while Mark used the NBA referee technique, signifying zero by holding up his fist. No worries, Brender, it's a cool photo to mark the milestone nonetheless.

Thirteen months later, the pattern of significant flights continued. Most of the previous year had been routine, but flight 1,100 was on Kenya Air from Nairobi to London, England. I was returning from another trip to Tanzania to climb Mount Kilimanjaro.

But big, round numbers or not, in terms of really unusual international flights, there will never be another like my 286th from Tokyo to Hong Kong. There can't be. The infamous Kai Tak (Kye-tock) Airport in HK was replaced soon after the British returned the territory to the Chinese in 1997. In October 1996, I basically spent my life savings to go over before the transfer occurred. I had always wanted to see Hong Kong, and no one had any idea what changes might take place once the Chinese took hold of this bastion of capitalism and one of the most beautiful cities in the world. I also had a connection with an old friend of the family, who had a connection with a local banker, who had a connection with a tailor near where I was staying, in the Tsim Sha Tsui district across the harbour. I'd stock up on some inexpensive designer suits for my upcoming career in hockey broadcasting.

After spending a few days in Tokyo with Japanese friends I knew from Hawaii, I enthusiastically boarded a United Airlines flight for Hong Kong. Aside from one drunk having to be restrained by the flight attendants, what really stands out was the approach into Kai Tak. I vaguely remembered watching a TV news magazine segment on the subject a few years before. I was abruptly reminded of it when a U.S. Air Force veteran sitting with his wife one row back asked me out of nowhere during the initial descent, "Ever flown into Kai Tak before?"

"No."

"Get ready."

"What?"

"It's crazy, man, we're gonna dive bomb."

"Dive bomb?"

"Oh yeah, wait 'til you see this descent. You come over some mountains, dive down, and level out through the neighbourhoods."

"What?" Dude was tickled to share this information.

Just then, our 747 went into a steep nosedive.

I didn't know whether to grip and lean forward with the momentum of my body weight or fight it, push on the armrests, and press my back against the seat. It was similar to coming off the highest point of a roller coaster, only in this case, the drop seemed to last a couple miles.

Steep descents are a necessity on occasion. Not steep descents like this. Finally, like that same roller coaster reaching the bottom of its drop, our plane just pulled up hard and levelled out, all in one amazingly smooth motion, as my innards sank into my seat. The drunk guy must have known what was coming.

Just moments after being able to breathe calmly again, we banked incredibly hard to the right, and I looked out the window at lights and buildings and streets rushing by, then we straightened out again, passing laundry on clotheslines strung between tenement buildings. We were looking straight out at the back porches of midrise buildings and at people's TV sets. We were flying *through* town at dusk. This probably didn't last as long as it seemed; we soon came to rest on the lone runway in Victoria Harbour. At the end of the runway, the plane pulled off to the side and parked. It was the first time I ever had to take one of those bizarre buses, with a door on each end and one on each side, from the tarmac to the terminal.

The Chinese spent a couple of billion dollars on a new airport and closed Kai Tak and ruined our fun in 1998. (In America, San Diego is the closest experience to this. Landing from the east, you briefly fly through a part of downtown below the top of some of the highest buildings.)

Flight 1,200 was significant, in that I had never flown to Sudbury, Ontario, before, and Porter Airlines took me there in January 2013. I was with co-producer/camera-gal Shannon Eckstein to shoot another hockey charity event, the donation of equipment to First Nations youngsters who otherwise wouldn't be able to play. The trip involved a "Sudbury Saturday Night" and a lot of tequila shots with Norm Flynn and the boys from Heroes Hockey. Consider me indoctrinated. We buzzed into the Sudbury Arena for a few minutes to take in a bit of a Wolves game. It's the absolute epitome of a classic Canadian junior hockey barn.

The shoot was for a program I produced and co-hosted called *Sports Access*, on AMI, or Accessible Media, a national TV and audio network in Canada that receives tax dollars to service the nation's blind and visually impaired audience. Added dialogue, description, and natural sound are key when catering to this audience, who have to be able to "see" every episode simply by listening.

Sports Access also focused on sports for impaired and disabled athletes at a time when that movement was starting to boom. In 2015, we wrapped up its fourth and final season where I was once again coordinating producer and occasional co-host. Production quality was very basic, based on the network's funding and infrastructure, but even with the limitations and an insanely tight schedule, we still managed to create AMI's most popular original series to date.

Outweighing all of the production and travel opportunities for me at AMI were the sheer number of inspirational stories in the blind and disabled sporting communities. Some of these remarkable features included a brother and sister who are totally blind and toss horseshoes in their yard on a breathtaking cove on the coast of Newfoundland, a blind skateboarder in Winnipeg, amputee sailors in Nova Scotia, watching a deaf-blind woman play hockey, blind triathletes training with sighted guides, sledge hockey players, wheelchair basketball players, high-school wrestlers and swimmers who are totally blind, and a hockey writer who is visually impaired, the list goes on and on. There were even blind downhill skiers who follow sighted guides down courses at 100 kilometres an hour while wearing walkie-talkie headsets.

Let's just say I was ready to run through a wall on countless occasions after watching someone do something completely ridiculous and inspiring, when you'd think they'd have no chance at all based on their physical limitation. Far more often, in fact, than the number of times I was inspired while covering the Maple Leafs those seasons, which I also did on a regular basis for the AMI audio channel.

Flight 1,300 was Chicago to Buffalo on Southwest in August 2014, flight 1,400 was Buffalo to Baltimore on Southwest in April 2015. Flight 1,500 was somewhat monumental. Air Canada took me from Montreal to Fredericton, New Brunswick, in March 2017, to provide live coverage of my first ever University Cup, the

Canadian version of an NCAA Frozen Four. Working with the Montreal Canadiens' excellent TV tandem of John Bartlett and Jason York, I was brought in to provide live insight and interviews from ice level.

Dropping in once or twice a season to handle a national television broadcast is a delight, but it's also the ultimate challenge. I'm not seeing the same team forty times, or the opponent for the third or fourth time. All of the TSN and Sportsnet telecasts I've been a part of during the last five years have essentially been one-offs, featuring rosters the crew had never seen before nor would likely see again. It definitely keeps preparation at a premium. Thankfully, most of these gigs have been play-by-play, my optimum role, and all of the shows have come off without a hitch. Doesn't hurt to be working with Cassie Campbell-Pascall, Louie DeBrusk, Craig Button, or Dave Reid.

Button and I did a Junior-A challenge championship game on TSN a few years back in Yarmouth, Nova Scotia. Surprisingly, the two Canadian teams both lost in the semis. The final was between Russia and the USA. Unexpectedly having to memorize an absurdly challenging Russian roster overnight was interesting to say the least. Often times I'll just study a roster over and over and over and repeat the names and numbers. In this case I actually made flashcards of the two teams, flipping through them time and again until the individual players and jerseys matched up in my brain.

The fact that these two opponents were facing off in the final actually made Craig and me chuckle. Who the hell in Canada was gonna watch *that* championship game?

In January 2015, I did an Ontario Hockey League

game in Ottawa while suffering with my first and (so far) only ever urinary tract infection. It kicked in during my flight to Ottawa. I had full-on nausea, cold sweats, and uncontrollable shivers the night before the game, slept little, and had a fever and dizziness during the telecast. I have no recollection whatsoever of the match, I just know I worked with Debrusk and Kyle Bukauskas and the first-time producer was happy with the show.

The University Cup semi-final and final in 2017 also featured a first-time producer. He did a great job. Me, I handled most everything pretty well for my first ice-level gig in three years, but I'll never forgive myself for screwing up the open of the final. If you were to pick the one thing you least wanted to screw up, it would be the open to the championship telecast. For no particular reason whatsoever, for the first time in my career, I decided not to ad lib and instead read part of the open over the video clips. I lost my spot on my notepad and flip-flopped some players' names. It drove me absolutely nuts.

My audio guy put it in perspective. "Hey, nobody died." Thanks. The rest of the telecast had to be flawless. I still think about that mistake — more often than I should. You can only hope the bosses remember the good stuff.

Here's to many more entertaining shows and to getting to 2,000 flights and beyond.

Fun landing at Kai Tak found on YouTube: Boeing 747 Hard Crosswind Landing Hong Kong

THE ICE-LEVEL MAN
COMETH (AND GOETH)

Coach Renney's words were prophetic. It was indeed the last time I did a Rangers game. In fact, as of the spring of 2017 it's the last time I've done a live NHL game telecast. November 1, 2008, marked the end of my ice-level existence on TV at the highest level of hockey. As is often the case for those holding the mic, destiny was determined by persons and circumstances beyond my control.

At MSG the TV Network, as in Madison Square Garden, one of the many business entities under the large MSG umbrella, there were generally four on-air people working a Rangers telecast at the home rink and three on the road. That didn't include the two or three people in the studio handling pre, post, and intermissions. As is still the case, Sam Rosen handled play-by-play, Joe Micheletti handled color commentary, John Giannone did the ice-level interviews and post-game scrums, while at home games, the iconic Al Trautwig would handle the live ice-level stuff between periods and bump Giannone to just post-game interview gathering.

Having just wrapped up three years in Boston, working as the ice-level guy for the Bruins on NESN (New England Sports Network), I was invited to be the emergency backup reporter on TV for Rangers games in New York. I was also dabbling in some work with the NHL Network based a bit uptown at NHL HQ on Sixth Avenue and also in Toronto.

Boston had been a tremendous experience, I felt I was on top of my game and, based on industry feedback, was one of the more efficient and knowledgeable third guys in the League. Aside from Paul Hendrick in Toronto, who is loaded with information and decades of experience, I felt I could match up my presentation with anyone's. It helped that I had hockey in my blood.

My brothers and I began skating and moving pucks on a pond in Michigan not long after we learned to walk. We all played house-league not far down the road and we were all religious Red Wings and NHL fans. My brothers played high-school hockey, I had quit playing and did play-by-play of the local games on our high-school radio station.

Of course, the always-frugal NESN had different ideas. TV boy, as I referred to myself, was about to get a little expensive entering his fourth season, and I was dumped.

Not renewed, more accurately, which was probably not a bad thing for my health as I had been living like a rock star.

Besides the cheap factor at NESN, where well-known on-air persons work for relative peanuts, it also didn't help that I refused to see eye-to-eye on all things with the network's executive producer (EP). At one point before my final season at NESN, the then-EP asked my co-producer Sarge Kerrisey and me to come up with a way to include reporter Naoko Funayama into a weekly segment on our successful Bruins half-hour magazine-style TV show *Rubber Biscuit*. Why, we had no idea. The extent of her on-air experience at that point had been covering sports on a local cable network in Maryland and as a part-time reporter at NESN to help translate with the Red Sox Japanese pitchers. Stylistically, it was an absolute mismatch, and given that *Rubber Biscuit* was often shot on-location during road trips and that I was also working an 82-game live hockey schedule while hosting and co-producing the show, we simply ignored the request. We weren't going to awkwardly ruin a really good program.

He also probably didn't like the fact that I was already producing and hosting a TV show on the side for EP Gord Cutler at the NHL Network.

Fast forward to the end of my final season. Who replaced me as ice-level reporter for the Bruins? Naoko Funayama of course. The EP apparently had his spite and/or revenge while the network had its savings. As it related to the loss of hockey background and entertainment for the fans, the network higher-ups didn't really care. They had no problem insulting the intelligence of Original Six fans. Period.

Taken in the early 2000s at the Air Canada
Centre, promoting my TV show, *Maple Leaf
America*, with Bob Harwood of Leafs TV.

This is how the TV business works sometimes.

Somewhat humbled, yet resilient, I had decent fall-back opportunities in the Big Apple. That's where the MSG opportunity unfolded. Through the small hockey world, I had a number of contacts in the market, including Rangers TV game producer Joe Whelan.

At one point in the off-season, it seemed I had a choice between being the full-time backup play-by-play guy on Rangers radio or being the backup reporter/anchor guy on TV. Joe encouraged me into the television gig.

Working with "The Maven" Stan Fischler in studio in New York, I had the chance to anchor a few Rangers and Islanders preseason and regular-season telecasts on MSG. Our job was pretty standard: we would sit at a fancy desk and discuss the teams on TV and toss back and forth with the talent on site. One of the strictest rules during the show came during the pregame warm-ups. When Giannone or Deb Placey, another ice-level reporter for the network, was standing on the bench to do the pre-game interview with a player and that player showed up, you immediately ended whatever conversation you were having and "threw" to the reporter at the rink. Under *no* circumstances would you make the player wait.

Studio show producer Paula McHale had been emphatic about this, and I distinctly remember cutting Stan off at one point to throw to Deb during the pre-game show of the Rangers–Columbus Blue Jackets game on October 25. From the studio host chair, you could see the bench shot on a monitor directly in front of you so there would be no delays. When Deb was done with the interview she threw back to us and we continued our conversation.

This was standard operating procedure, and during my first-ever on-air regular season Rangers game at the Joe Louis Arena in Detroit, things went swimmingly. Talk about a cool deal. My first regular season gig for the "Blueshirts" was against my childhood team back in my hometown. I had been there once with the Bruins previously, on March 11, 2007, but that game was on a Sunday afternoon and handled by NBC as a national game of the week, so NESN was bumped and I didn't broadcast the match. Rangers–Red Wings on October 18, 2008, became my first-ever telecast from the Joe.

(During my three years in Boston, the league played what was called an imbalanced schedule, with each team playing every division rival six times a season with the rest of the Bruins' schedule weighted to the Eastern Conference. Detroit was in the Western Conference at the time, didn't play Boston in 2005–06 at all, had the one game at the Joe in 2007, and played *at* Boston in February 2008. I actually did a book signing with Hall of Fame linesman Ray "Scampy" Scapinello at the Joe during the 2007 game because I knew I didn't have to work it. We signed copies of our book *Between the Lines*.)

The Rangers–Red Wings telecast went very well. The format called for a sit-down walk-off in the first intermission with Ranger Markus Naslund. A question or two longer than a typical hockey-intermission interview, it was done in chairs in "Al Trautwig" fashion: very conversational, very relaxed. Second intermission, I did a standing three-question interview with Red Wings defenceman Nicklas Lidstrom that also went very well. *Like riding a bike*, I'm thinking; I was back where I left off in Beantown.

The Rangers lost in overtime, 5–4, we chartered back to New York, and the reviews were good. Maybe they were too good.

The following week, I was in-studio with Stan for that Columbus game, eating pizza and watching hockey when we weren't on the air.

One week later, Saturday, November 1, I was back on the road, this time in Toronto at the Air Canada Centre, Rangers against the Leafs. It would be eventful and memorable from start to finish.

The unbelievable, the unfathomable, a mystery to this day, occurred during the pregame warm-ups, as I stood on the Rangers bench preparing to interview defenceman Dan Girardi, selected by our producer because he grew up nearby.

Standard operating procedure at the bench; the players hop on the ice, the guy who is slated to be interviewed usually takes one or two laps around the end zone and then heads over to talk. That's exactly what Girardi did. As was customary, Deb Placey, the in-studio host in this case, would wrap up her conversation with the analyst and throw to me as soon as she saw us.

"Hey, Dan," I said to Girardi as he skated over and stood next to me. "Ready to go in a sec." I quickly reviewed the two or three questions in my head as I listened to Deb in my earpiece.

Instead, after the analyst finished his comments (I honestly don't recall who was in-studio that night with Deb), Placey went ahead and asked her sidekick another question.

"Dude, she just asked another question. Hang on a second, we'll get it out here," I told Girardi, who was immediately impatient and annoyed. Why wouldn't he be, the clock is ticking and warm-up time is limited. Our interview should have started, and I was getting uncomfortable. "Joe, what happened," I said into the mic, communicating with Whelan in our production truck at the ACC. "She needs to bring it out."

I could hear "program" in my IFB (interruptible feedback), a fancy acronym for earpiece, "program" being the on-air conversation from the studio in New York. The analyst seemed to be in no rush. After a minute that seemed like ten, he finally started to wind down, and I told Girardi, "Okay, stand by."

But when the analyst wrapped up his latest thought, Placey went ahead and asked him *another* question.

I held the mic to my chest to muffle it and said to Girardi, "She just asked another question. I don't know what's going on." F-bombs were on the tip of my tongue.

Even if you think or know you're not "hot," you never swear around a live mic, just in case. Girardi wasn't really concerned about my dilemma, to him this was just an absolutely unnecessary delay, and I was the douchebag creating it. He skated away, took a slap shot from the right point, and then skated back. During this, I was trying to reach Joe, who didn't respond. "What is going on, Joe, Girardi is losing it. Why didn't she send it out?"

There was some panic in my head, but this being my third game with a new network, I was trying to stay cool. Didn't want to yell, definitely didn't want to swear at the truck through the mic. But this was bullshit. Girardi returned just in time for me to hear Deb ask yet another question. The conversation continued in my ear from New York, and no one was doing anything about it.

I was then speaking stream of consciousness to Girardi and Joe at the same time. "I don't know what to say, they just keep on talking. They're not throwing it out here. I say just bag it. Joe, can we just bag this, they're not throwing it out here. Girardi's gotta go!" Nothing.

In almost forty years of broadcasting, I've never been as stressed out before or since. Meanwhile, the *Hockey Night in Canada* crew handling the Leafs telecast that night had come and gone. They actually conducted live interviews on both benches in the time I was standing around waiting.

After the fourth Q and A back in the studio, Deb finally threw it to me. The interview was flat — he couldn't pretend to give a shit — and I kept it quick. Girardi had missed out on four or five minutes of warm-up. He was pissed, and I had a feeling I'd be hearing about it later. The camera guy and Eddie, the ice-level stage manager, both with me on the bench, looked at each other in disbelief.

The Rangers took a 1–0 lead with ten seconds remaining in the first period. Ryan Callahan scored the goal while Dan Girardi had one of the assists. Yeah baby, who needs warm-up?

We didn't interview a player involved in the scoring on the goal as we had already decided upon Scott Gomez as our walk-off guest. I actually lobbied for him to be the guy because of a familiarity factor. "Gomer" and I had a joke-around acquaintanceship that went back to his New Jersey days and my Boston days for whatever reason. He'd make fun of my clothes; I'd respond by saying, "You *wish* you had this tie."

Our interaction in Toronto that night garnered this response from sports media reporter Phil Mushnick the next day in the *New York Post*.

It's rare when an NHL player removes his game face during a between-periods interview. But after one in Rangers–Leafs Saturday, new MSG rink-side reporter Rob Simpson (last stop, Bruins games on NESN) interviewed Scott Gomez, who quit — midanswer — to tell Simpson: "I'm kinda distracted by your outfit. Anything match there?"

At interview's close, Gomez again poked at Simpson's clothing. "Halloween's over," he said.

Simpson, wearing a tie, white shirt and what appeared

to be a blazer — nothing out of the ordinary, though MSG never provided a head-to-toe shot — seemed confused. The session seemed more odd than funny.

Phil had no idea this had been a running joke with Gomer, and I obviously wasn't confused, but I also wasn't ready in my second road game with MSG to take it the next level by saying, "You *wish* you had this tie," to end the conversation. Whelan was a bit of a temperamental producer to say the least and he preferred to play things pretty straight. In hindsight, I probably shouldn't have curbed the familiarity and personality that came naturally, but unfortunately I did. I didn't know I'd be getting yelled at either way.

Blair Betts scored his second goal of the season to give the Rangers a 2–0 lead after two periods. Warm-up shmarm-up.

Second intermission I interviewed former (and future) Ranger Dominic Moore. In what was kind of a nervy manoeuver, I asked about the health of his brother Steve, who with the Colorado Avalanche had suffered career-ending injuries via a brutal on-ice attack by Vancouver Canuck Todd Bertuzzi back in 2004. Steve was out of hockey and lawsuits related to the incident were dragging on. Dom, Steve, and a third brother Mark had all played college hockey together at Harvard. He didn't mind the questions — it was a thoughtful conversation — and off we all went to the third period.

Good on-cams, 2–0 Rangers lead, I'm thinking maybe we need to fuck up the pregame interview more often.

Or maybe not.

Twelve minutes into the third period, the Maple Leafs

went nuts. First, rookie John Mitchell scored to put the home team on the board. One minute and twenty-six seconds later, Jason Blake scored to tie the game. Fifty-two seconds later, defenceman Pavel Kubina scored. A minute and two seconds later, Mitchell scored again. Then, to bring the cluster fuck full circle, Dominic Moore scored with two minutes left in the game. New York goalie Steve Valiquette was shell-shocked; Toronto won 5–2.

Holy shit.

I started the post-game media scrum with Rangers head coach Tom Renney by phrasing the question: "How exactly did the trolley come off the tracks?" I thought it was a clever way of asking, "How exactly did your team completely screw this up?" Whelan the producer didn't like the phraseology. He felt it wasn't serious enough. Not sure about Renney, but literally every New York paper used his answer the next morning: "The trolley came off the tracks because . . ." I had written the metaphor for everyone and felt validated for using the terminology.

An evening of misfortune continued.

Chartering out of Toronto, we literally puddle jumped Lake Ontario and landed in Buffalo to go through immigration privately. We all disembarked and lined up, coaches first from the front of the plane, media and staff next from the middle, and then the players from the back. The coaching staff passed the U.S. border agents and headed back on the plane. Next up was the media, each of us ready to pass by one of two computers, me at the head of the line on the left, Whelan at the head of the line on the right.

That's when the computers malfunctioned. They could no longer read our passports. For the next twenty minutes,

Joe and I stood at the front of a line that wasn't moving. Of course, the players saw only the tall douchebag who had delayed Girardi during pregame once again fucking things up. They didn't know anything about the computers going down — no one was talking. It was dead quiet. They also didn't notice Whelan so much; he's a foot shorter than the "new guy" Donkey Balls. They probably didn't even realize there were two computers; they just saw the freakishly tall dimwit looking uncomfortable at the front of the line.

I remember searching back over the line and seeing Valiquette at the very end of it. He shot me a look full of daggers. Dude was tired, just got smoked for five goals in the third period, and now some likely criminal broadcast nob was wanted by the feds. Why else would we be standing here?

Mercifully, the immigration guys gave up on the computers and let us board with just a quick glance at the passports. I was first on ahead of Joe and while walking past Renney I quickly let him know what had happened.

In passing, I said, "The computers fried; they just let us on now." That's when he hit me with the news that essentially meant "enjoy this ride because it's your last."

I kind of wasn't sure I had heard him utter, "This is your last Rangers game," or maybe it was just wishful thinking I hadn't heard it. Or, perhaps, knowing that none of the bullshit over the course of the evening was actually my doing, I was confident the truth would come out and I'd be just fine.

It never did.

On the way out of the Westchester Airport after stopping to take a leak, I was chatting with Scott Gomez as

I walked. Whelan, who was kind enough to share his car service with me back to the city, took exception to what looked like me wasting time while needlessly fraternizing. When I sat down in the back, he laid into me with every expletive in the book six times over. It was mostly about making him wait, but there was a little in there about my post-game "trolley" question. He said nothing about the pregame. Oddly enough, after he cooled down a few minutes later, he actually complimented me on my work.

A couple weeks later, while standing in the Zamboni corner near the glass at Madison Square Garden, Al Trautwig said something like, "You'll be alright, Simmer, you'll always have hockey."

John Gianonne, like Trautwig, a true pro, said something along the same lines: good luck, you're a hockey guy, you'll be fine. Apparently they knew something I didn't. My days at MSG as a back-up, and any hopes of becoming a staffer, were over.

This is how the TV business works sometimes.

Naoko went on to handle the ice-level reporting on NESN until the spring of 2013. I understand she is doing freelance work in Massachusetts and New Hampshire.

John Gianonne and Deb Placey still do ice-level for MSG. Joe Whelan and the network parted ways in 2012. In 2017, Joe landed the gig producing the Columbus Blue Jackets telecasts.

Me on YouTube, doing God's work: Simpson Live Demo

At ECW Press, we want you to enjoy this book in whatever format you like, whenever you like. Leave your print book at home and take the eBook to go! Purchase the print edition and receive the eBook free. Just send an email to ebook@ecwpress.com and include:

- the book title
- the name of the store where you purchased it
- your receipt number
- your preference of file type: PDF or ePub

A real person will respond to your email with your eBook attached. And thanks for supporting an independently owned Canadian publisher with your purchase!

ROB SIMPSON is one of the only human beings in the last five years to bridge the rivalry between TSN and Rogers Sportsnet, having done live TV reporting and play-by-play for both. Formerly the host of *NHL Live* in New York, Simpson co-hosts an international radio talk show while residing in Toronto. Find him on Twitter @simmerpuck.